UNSHAKEN
ALLEGIANCE

Living wisely as Christians with
diminishing religious freedoms

PATRICK PARKINSON

matthiasmedia
SYDNEY · YOUNGSTOWN

Matthias Media
(St Matthias Press Ltd ACN 067 558 365)
Email: info@matthiasmedia.com.au
Internet: matthiasmedia.com.au
Please visit our website for current postal and telephone contact information.

Matthias Media (USA)
Email: sales@matthiasmedia.com
Internet: matthiasmedia.com
Please visit our website for current postal and telephone contact information.

All websites cited in this book were accessed on 24 February 2025.

ISBN 978 1 922980 49 6

Cover design by Carol Lam.
Typesetting by Lankshear Design.

"I am coming to you now, but I say these things while I am still in the world, so that they may have the full measure of my joy within them. I have given them your word and the world has hated them, for they are not of the world any more than I am of the world."
(John 17:13–14)

Jesus said, "My kingdom is not of this world. If it were, my servants would fight to prevent my arrest by the Jewish leaders. But now my kingdom is from another place."
(John 18:36)

Therefore, since we are receiving a kingdom that cannot be shaken, let us be thankful, and so worship God acceptably with reverence and awe, for our "God is a consuming fire."
(Heb 12:28–29)

Highly regarded US Supreme Court Justice Clarence Thomas once explained that the art of great legal writing is "to put a ten-dollar idea in a five-cent sentence". In other words, there are skilled ways to put important things in language that's accessible. That is exactly what Patrick Parkinson has done in this book. Drawing on law, politics, culture and theology, Parkinson not only provides an astute overview of the great challenges facing our times, but—crucially—he also offers a clear and practical roadmap on how to respond well as faithful Christians.

Paul Coleman, Executive Director, Alliance Defending Freedom International

Patrick Parkinson has done us a great service in writing this book. The relationship between Christians and the law, particularly laws around religious freedom, is changing rapidly in the West. Parkinson helps us to navigate the challenges that these changes bring with his typically clear and measured approach. He knows his law and his Bible, and integrates the two with wisdom, practical advice and careful consideration of both domains. This book is a must-read for any Christian who is in public life, or who wonders whether their Christian convictions might put them at odds with the law.

The Right Rev Dr Richard Condie, Anglican Bishop of Tasmania

Professor Patrick Parkinson's book is a must-read for Christians who want to understand the rising challenges to religious freedom, and how to respond when obedience to God brings us into conflict with the law of the land. Patrick has a rare talent to make complex legal issues both comprehensible and engaging. *Unshaken Allegiance* is a timely wake-up call; for too long we have taken for granted the freedom to practise our faith, and we need to prepare ourselves for adverse headwinds to come. I wholeheartedly commend this book to you.

The Right Reverend Dr Michael Stead, Anglican Bishop of South Sydney, Chair of Freedom for Faith

We are most fortunate that Professor Patrick Parkinson's expertise in law and public policy has been marshalled in the cause of religious freedom. This lucid and practical guide to the legal pitfalls lying in wait for those in active public Christian service will be a most valuable resource for many years.

Rex Ahdar, Emeritus Professor of Law, University of Otago, New Zealand

Patrick Parkinson has written a timely and courageous book that tackles one of the most pressing issues of our era: the erosion of religious freedom in post-Christian societies. With clarity and compassion, he equips Christians to navigate legal and cultural pressures with both wisdom and faith.

This is a vital resource for church leaders and believers alike who are seeking to understand the shifting legal and cultural landscape. Parkinson offers not only expert and experienced legal insight but deep pastoral concern in urging the church to respond with integrity and courage.

Unshaken Allegiance is both a wake-up call and a guidebook. Drawing on decades of legal and Christian service, Parkinson helps readers grasp the real challenges facing people of faith today, and shows us how to live faithfully—even when the law may not always be our ally.

David Hodson OBE KC (Hons) MCIArb, Honorary Professor of Law, University of Leicester

This book identifies fast-moving and dangerous illiberal trends in Western culture. This cultural progressivism poses a direct threat to free speech, which is, in turn, a big challenge for the Church. There needs to be a strong push-back against this new illiberalism, and Patrick Parkinson's book helps us to understand what is happening and what to do next.

Martin Charlesworth, Founder of Jubilee+, United Kingdom

CONTENTS

INTRODUCTION

A Christian and a lawyer?

After I finished my undergraduate law degree at an English university, I spent nine months behind the Iron Curtain in Bratislava, Czechoslovakia (now the capital of Slovakia). This was 1981–82. Officially, I was a British Council scholar in socialist family law under an educational exchange agreement between the UK and the Soviet bloc countries of Eastern Europe. Martial law had been declared in neighbouring Poland, and the communist governments of Eastern Europe were cracking down on dissent.

This period gave me the opportunity to share fellowship with my Christian brothers and sisters as they endured considerable difficulty. They were free to worship, but going to church virtually ensured that certain jobs or promotions were not open to them. This was particularly so for Catholics, who might go to church in another community some distance away where they were less likely to be recognized. People could be Christians, but to speak openly about one's faith at work or in the university was to invite trouble. I knew people who had been 'secret believers' in order to try to keep their jobs. The churches were carefully controlled by the government. Students could study theology and become pastors or priests, but the study of Marxism-Leninism was mandatory, and so they had to pass an examination in atheism. To be a pastor or priest required government approval.

My time in Bratislava gave me opportunities to share my faith quietly with students in the university accommodation provided to me. These students came from many parts of the world where the Soviet Union had influence at the time, such as Afghanistan, the communist countries of South-East Asia, and parts of Africa. Most were countries that were otherwise closed to the gospel. These students took some risks to speak to me about faith, but they were utterly disillusioned with communism, and this fuelled their interest in Christianity. The Christian faith offered a real alternative to belief in the regime.

During that time, I had connections with a remarkable Catholic underground movement. Students met secretly in weekly Bible-study groups in every Faculty of Comenius University. They shared Christian books, such as John Stott's *Basic Christianity*, which were translated into the Slovak language and smuggled in from the West. They also passed around what was known as 'samizdat literature', articles written on a typewriter using carbon paper. Before the days of photocopiers or desktop computers, this allowed them to create up to ten legible copies for sharing.

The Slovak Christians could not have been more welcoming, but one thing about me they could not understand: how could I be a Christian *and* a lawyer? For them, this was a contradiction in terms. Law, to the Slovaks, was indistinguishable from government, and government was indistinguishable from the Communist Party. To be a lawyer, or even to get into law school, meant being in good standing with the Party. The idea that the courts might somehow be independent from government, or that they might apply the law impartially when government interests were involved, was entirely incomprehensible.

By way of contrast, it was unthinkable to English Christians that the law would *not* be independent. The rule of law—the idea that governments exercise authority only insofar as the law allows—is deeply rooted in English history. It has its intellectual origins in Christian thought. God gives us rulers, but at the same time their authority is limited. Religious freedom was also deeply ingrained in the English tradition, as it is in many other countries of the English-speaking world and beyond. For me, there was no contradiction between being a lawyer and a Christian.

A growing convergence

Yet over the last forty years or so, there has been the beginnings of convergence between the state of religious freedom in Western countries and the experience of the Eastern European Christians with whom I lived and shared fellowship all those years ago. I must emphasize that we are seeing only the beginnings of this convergence. My friends in Slovakia risked their jobs and even their freedom for the sake of the gospel. Three leaders of the Catholic underground movement died in suspicious circumstances in the year before I was there. Almost certainly, they were murdered by the secret police. We are not in such a dire place, nor in most respects are we remotely close to it.

And yet, the experience of ordinary Christians is, perhaps, not so dissimilar.

As a university law professor working in Australia, I certainly experienced discrimination from colleagues because of my faith— so much so that when I applied for a senior position at the University of Sydney, where I had been teaching for 15 years by then, the Vice-Chancellor felt he had to provide a categorical assurance at the interview that my faith was not an impediment to my appointment to that role. No-one minded me having a private faith; it was because I spoke about it *publicly* that opposition arose. That was not so different from the position of Christians in Czechoslovakia. They could live out their faith, just as long as they didn't talk about it—which, of course, is a contradiction in terms for a Bible-believing Christian.

A few years later, another Vice-Chancellor told me of a female academic in an area of the sciences where there were very few women. She was also not of Anglo-Australian heritage. She told him that in all the years she had worked in this field, she had never experienced discrimination as a woman. But as a Christian? Well, that was a different story.

Some of the discrimination that Christians experience is not directly due to their faith. Teachers lose their jobs because they are unwilling to affirm that the mentally troubled child who yesterday was male is now female. People are discriminated against because they once opposed the legalization of same-sex marriage, or because they find it difficult to go along with their corporation's new-found social justice cause, which all people who want to succeed in the business must now embrace. Medical specialists may find it difficult to work in certain areas because they cannot accept requirements that violate their Christian ethics. These are all forms of discrimination that are associated with religious beliefs, if not directly forms of religious discrimination. The Eastern European Christians found that some jobs were not open to them because of their faith. Being a lawyer was just one example. Increasingly, Christians in the West are experiencing similar issues.

Diminishing religious freedom

It is now also part of our experience for laws to constrain our religious freedom in various ways. Of course this varies from one country to another. But it is not uncommon for laws to restrict the right of faith-based organizations to select, or prefer to select, staff who share their beliefs. They may get into trouble with anti-discrimination laws in other ways where there is a conflict between the moral values of the organization and secular values enshrined in anti-discrimination laws. It may be unlawful, for example, to discriminate against an employee or applicant for employment because of their "lawful sexual conduct", however much the person's sexual morals and practices differ from what the New Testament teaches.

It is possible also for individual Christians to find that they are accused of "hate speech" because of statements they have made that reflect mainstream Christian beliefs, or because someone regards their social-media post as offensive. Even in those countries with quite robust constitutional protections for freedom of religion and speech, Christians may find that those protections only go so far. They constrain what Congress or Parliament can enact, but they may not constrain how private universities restrict freedom of speech. They may not affect what limitations employers impose on employees concerning their speech outside of the context of their employment. They may not affect the litmus tests that are used for job applicants to ensure the business does not have too much diversity of opinion in relation to the organization's 'values'.

No, this is not persecution—at least in terms of physical suffering. No, Christians in Western democracies are not in anything like the same position as in countries where Christians are severely constrained even in attending church. We should not exaggerate the difficulties. Most Christians in the West will live ordinary lives without experiencing serious adverse consequences because of their faith (although many may find themselves reviled or maligned, as Jesus warned).[1] But the persecution of the few has a chilling effect on the many. Without anyone necessarily telling us to do so, we become secret believers, at least in our workplaces or schools and universities. The spread of the gospel is constrained because we are fearful of the consequences of being known as those who follow Jesus.

For these times

This is a book about these times, and for these times. It is about how we live as good citizens of our countries but with an allegiance to another King—a King whose demands must, in certain situations, take precedence over the requirements of the law. It is a book about how we navigate a world in which laws may be increasingly weaponized against us, against our churches, or against the Christian organizations in which we work. The book draws upon 15 years of experience in arguing the case for religious freedom as a co-founder and sometime chair of Freedom for Faith, a Christian legal think-tank that acts as a peak voice to government on religious freedom in Australia.[2]

It is not, to be clear, a book that offers legal advice. I will provide numerous examples of laws that may impact upon religious freedom or freedom of speech from various countries, in particular Australia, New Zealand and the UK. But the law varies from one country to another, and in those countries that are divided into states or provinces—such as Australia, the USA and Canada—the law will vary from one state or province to the next. Furthermore, by

---

1   See, for example, Matthew 5:11-12. See also P Grimmond, *Suffering Well: The predictable surprise of Christian suffering*, Matthias Media, 2011, chapter 6.
2   See freedomforfaith.org.au.

the time you read this book, it is possible that the law on an issue might have changed. If you need specific legal advice, consult a lawyer who can offer advice tailored to your circumstances and your jurisdiction.

Apart from being a book about the law, written by a law professor, this is also a book about Christian discipleship. Throughout the book, especially in the second half, I will draw upon the Bible's teachings on how we should live. I will suggest ways in which those teachings can be applied both in circumstances where we experience legal difficulties, and in order to avoid legal difficulties in the first place.

As Christian citizens, we should be law-abiding; we should submit to governments, as both Paul and Peter make clear in their writings. However, it is important to think about what compliance with the law means and does not mean in modern circumstances. These are very different from New Testament times. Therefore, I will also explore how we can work out when it is right to disobey a law because it conflicts with the demands of our Christian faith.

I am not a theologian, so readers who come to the book seeking a theological work may well be disappointed. There is much more that could be said on the relationship between God and government, drawing upon theology, philosophy and the history of political ideas. Much has been written on these issues by people much more learned in those issues than I.[3] This is intended as a practical book, written especially for pastors and other leaders of churches or Christian organizations, as well as for everyone interested in what it means to be citizens both of an earthly nation and of Jesus' kingdom at a time when the tide of religious freedom is receding.

The first four chapters explain the problem—how laws now constrict religious freedom in many Western countries in ways that

---

3   Recent books include NT Wright and MF Bird, *Jesus and the Powers: Christian political witness in an age of totalitarian terror and dysfunctional democracies* (Zondervan, 2024); MP Jensen, *Subjects and Citizens: The politics of the gospel: Lessons from Romans 12–15* (Matthias Media, 2024); W Grudem, *Politics According to the Bible: A comprehensive resource for understanding modern political issues in light of Scripture* (Zondervan, 2017).

were unknown in the past, and why the law has tended to develop in these ways. Chapter 5 explores faith perspectives on our current situation.

Chapter 6 then examines the limitations on our Christian duty to obey the law. Chapters 7–10 deal with some of the issues that now arise for us as Christians: what it means to comply with different kinds of law, and how we decide when not to comply; how we can avoid unnecessary legal trouble; how we resolve issues quickly when there is potential for legal conflict; and when it is necessary and appropriate to stand on our legal rights. The final chapter looks to the future.

Not all these chapters will be equally relevant to every reader. While I have endeavoured not to be overly technical in my descriptions and analysis of the law, some of my explanations may tax the patience of some readers while being helpful to others.

My thanks to various friends who were kind enough to read chapters of the book. John Watson of Good Mahi gave me information about the example of Bethlehem College in New Zealand (chapter 8). Thanks also to my editor, Geoff Robson of Matthias Media, who provided very useful feedback throughout. Of course, any errors are my own, as are all points of view expressed.

PART I

UNDERSTANDING
THE PROBLEM

1

WHEN LAW BECOMES A SOURCE OF OPPRESSION

*Does God require us to obey the laws
of oppressive regimes?*

Traffic lights

There is a highway in Chechnya, a republic that forms part of Russia. This highway has a traffic light that is permanently on red.[1] The traffic light is in perfect working order. It does exactly what it is meant to do. Each day, thousands of people drive through this red light to travel from one region to another. The locals have little choice but to break the law to get where they need to go for their ordinary business.

For the great majority, there will be no consequences. However, the red traffic light gives the authorities the right to prosecute any user of this highway for running a red light if the authorities choose to do so. If there is an accident involving a local villager who collides with someone in a position of power, it will always be the villager's fault, for he or she ran a red light.

This is an area in which there are a lot of powerful people. It is close to the village of Akhmat Kurt, the native home of Chechen

---

1   K Galeev, 'On a highway leading from Chechnya to Dagestan there is ...' [X post], 23 November 2022 (x.com/kamilkazani/status/1595456040677556226).

leader Ramzan Kadyrov, a close ally of Russian President Vladimir Putin. The village is one of Kadyrov's strongholds, and he runs Chechnya as a personal fiefdom. He has weaponized the law for use as a means of exerting power.

In democratic societies, we are not used to the idea that law could be weaponized in this way. It is far from uncommon for us to be frustrated by traffic lights—sometimes intensely frustrated. We are the 18th car in a queue waiting to turn into a main road, but the traffic light turns green only long enough to allow three cars through the junction. We may rail at the stupidity of the people who programmed the traffic light and who provided such a limited opportunity for people to turn into the main road. We might even risk running a red light, hoping that it stays on amber long enough to allow us through; but we do not seriously doubt the integrity of the programmer of those lights. We accept that he or she is sincerely motivated by a desire to regulate the traffic effectively.

Law, in democratic societies, is not a means of exercising arbitrary power. It regulates the society for its good in myriad ways. The courts have some degree of independence from government, inasmuch as judges are meant to enforce the law without fear or favour, whatever the status of the defendant, and without being beholden to the will of the government. In many countries, prosecutorial authorities are independent and make judgements on whether to prosecute on a professional basis, without influence from government, or from family or friends of the alleged perpetrator.

And that's the way it should be.

Law as a means of oppression

However, there is nothing in the nature of a legal system that requires it to be benign. Law can be used as a means of oppression, and often is. Law in Nazi Germany offers an illustration of how an existing and well-established legal system can be gradually adapted to fulfil the government's desire to control the population.

Two fundamental principles of a just legal system existed in Germany before the Nazis came to power, but were gradually eroded.

The first is the principle that criminal laws should not be retrospective—that is, someone should not be punished for conduct that was not a crime at the time the conduct occurred. The second is that the law should be clear about what is being prohibited. Citizens should know what that law forbids so they can obey it.

In the first phase of Nazi rule, Hitler's government departed from the principle against retrospectivity. For example, a 1934 law extended the death penalty to certain crimes committed in 1933. Laws passed in that year also retroactively legalized various decrees and acts. Then in 1935, section 2 of the German Penal Code was amended to allow for prosecutions of conduct that deserved punishment "according to the sound feeling of the people". If no penal statute could directly be applied to such a 'crime', it was to be punished according to whatever statute was most analogous. It also became an offence to slander the National Socialist Party. Gradually, the law's independence was eroded, and the whole machinery of law stood at the service of the leader.[2]

One of the ways in which law can be used as a tool of oppression is through the enacting of vague statutes that give the police and prosecutors enormous discretion and opportunity to target people who are perceived to be enemies of the regime. Section 2 of the German Penal Code was a law of that kind. It allowed the government to decide what conduct fell within the terms of the statute; and while there were courts that had some degree of independence from government, such was the comprehensive power of the Nazis by the late 1930s that the judge hearing a case was likely to be a supporter of the regime.

Law as a means of silencing dissent

Just as law can be a means of oppression, so too it can be used to stifle dissent. In 2002, Russia enacted its Federal Law on Combating Extremist Activity. On paper, the law's intent is commendable—it

---

2   For more on this, see F Neumann, *The Rule of Law: Political theory and the legal system in modern society*, Berg, 1986.

seeks to protect the Russian people from terrorism and other violent extremist activity. It also claims to operate within the bounds of "recognition of, respect for and protection of human and civil rights and freedoms and also of the lawful interests of organizations".[3] This might be taken as an indirect reference to the Russian Constitution, where Article 28 states:

> Everyone shall be guaranteed freedom of conscience and religion, including the right to profess individually or collectively any religion or not to profess any religion, and freely to choose, possess and disseminate religious and other convictions and act in accordance with them.[4]

However, in practice this legislation has been wielded to silence dissent, notably against religious minorities. Jehovah's Witnesses, for example, have been branded an "extremist" organization.[5] The group, which requires pacifism of its members, was accused of undermining state sovereignty and inciting religious discord. By the end of 2019, according to the United States Commission on International Religious Freedom, "hundreds of [Jehovah's Witnesses] remained in detention, had travel restrictions imposed upon them, or were under investigation".[6]

How different are the legal systems of democratic societies?

A permanently red traffic light in a remote corner of Russia may seem of little relevance to Christians in democratic societies; and it

---

3   From the English translation provided by the European Commission for Democracy through Law, 24 February 2012 (venice.coe.int/webforms/documents/default. aspx?pdffile=CDL-REF(2012)012-e).
4   See the translation of the Russian Constitution available at Constitute: constituteproject.org/constitution/Russia_2014.
5   See J Slotkin, 'Top Russian court bans Jehovah's Witnesses, claiming "extremist activities"', *NPR*, 20 April 2017 (npr.org/sections/thetwo-way/2017/04/20/524906703/ top-russian-court-bans-jehovah-s-witnesses-under-anti-extremism-law).
6   United States Commission on International Religious Freedom, '2020 Annual Report', April 2020 (uscirf.gov/publications/2020-annual-report).

is true that we don't experience such shameless exercises of arbitrary power as in Chechnya, nor such use of the legal system to harass or imprison dissenters as occurred in Nazi Germany. While we have laws against terrorism and other offences against national security, such laws in Western democracies allow room for public protest and dissent.

In Western democracies, legislation is passed by democratically elected parliaments with a mandate to enact laws that enhance the common good. We may disagree with some of those laws—that is our right and privilege in a democratic society. However, we have reason for confidence, do we not, that if laws were used in the way they were in Nazi Germany, or in countless other autocratic regimes, the courts would act as a bulwark for our liberties. And even if the courts were compromised (for the government appoints the judges), would not voters have the final say, every few years, about whether a government that erects permanent red lights should continue in office?

Generally, yes. Compared to countries such as Russia, North Korea or Iran, or a host of other autocratic societies that could be named, people in democratic societies are relatively free. Traditions of liberty and respect for human rights run deep, and in many places these values are embedded in the constitutional structures of the country.

However, as Christians we have no right to assume that the law in our country will stay this way. We live in a time when adherence to faith is receding across the Western world, when committed Christians with an active church involvement are becoming an ever-smaller minority of the population. In many European countries that have had a strong Christian heritage, most people either have no identification with faith or adhere to another religious faith. That is true also of Australia, New Zealand and Canada. In several European countries, including the UK, 10 per cent or less of the population say that religion is very important in their lives.[7]

These countries could justifiably be described as post-Christian societies—those which were once premised on Christian beliefs and

---

7   J Evans, 'Where is the most religious place in the world?' *Pew Research Center*,
     9 August 2024 (pewresearch.org/short-reads/2024/08/09/where-is-the-most-
     religious-place-in-the-world).

values, but which are no longer. Societies that have emerged from a history of strong Christian commitment may now be post-Christian to a greater or lesser degree.

A useful proxy for seeing how far a society has strayed from traditional Christian values is to look at the rate of births outside marriage. In parts of northern Europe, including England and Wales, more than half of all births are to parents who are not married to one another, a proportion of which (typically about a third) are not even living together at the time of birth.[8] The figure is over 40 percent in the USA. The proportion of first children born to women who are not married is even higher. They may have one child out of wedlock and, a few years later, have more children within a marriage.

The decline in religious freedom

At the same time as the tide of religious faith is going out, so too the tide of religious freedom is going out. This is a paradox, for human rights have become something of a replacement religious creed in post-Christian societies. Yet, even in some societies where governments express great commitment to human rights, respect for at least some human rights is receding quickly. This is especially so in terms of the core freedoms of speech, religion, association and conscience, insofar as they clash, or might appear to clash, with ideas about equality, non-discrimination, and the protection of favoured minorities (more on this in chapter 4).

In the last three years in parts of Australia, for example, we have seen laws passed by democratically elected governments that:

- prohibit prayer with another person about certain matters
- expose Christian schools to the risk of being sued for discrimination if they insist on appointing, or even preferring, staff who have a Christian commitment

---

8   See, for example, J Pinkstone, 'More babies born out of wedlock than into married families for first time on record', *The Telegraph*, 9 August 2022 (telegraph.co.uk/news/2022/08/09/babies-born-wedlock-2021-first-time-record).

- make it very difficult for Christian organizations to require staff to maintain certain moral standards in the areas of sexual activity and family life.[9]

Laws of this kind are also being passed in other countries.[10]

The decline in freedom of speech

Even laws which are, on their face, neutral can be used to harass people who dissent from a particular viewpoint or ideology. Because Christian views and values are now offensive to many, laws that prohibit offensive speech may be used to target people of faith who express opinions that are not institutionally favoured.

Laws making it punishable to cause offence to others are proliferating in several countries. In the United States, with robust protections for freedom of speech and religion in the First Amendment to the Constitution, the courts are likely to be a bulwark against interference with basic liberties. However, protection for freedom of speech elsewhere is not as robust, which allows for the proliferation of such laws. There is enormous scope for provisions about causing offence to be used as a pretext for action against those who express points of view that some find offensive.

Consider, for example, section 127 of the *Communications Act 2003* in the UK. This makes it an offence to send "by means of a public electronic communications network a message or other matter that is grossly offensive or of an indecent, obscene or menacing character". In December 2022, James Goddard received a letter from a police officer attached to London's Public Order Crime Team.[11] Goddard had posted a ten-second video of Wembley Way, a road leading to England's national football stadium, which was lined with a corridor of colourful 'Progress Pride Flags' to mark the Pride movement's 50th anniversary. Most of the video simply showed him walking up the

9   These will be discussed in detail in chapter 2.
10   See chapters 2 and 3.
11   'UK police want to interview man over his Twitter commentary on video of pride flags', *Free Republic*, 7 January 2023 (freerepublic.com/focus/f-chat/4123091/posts).

road, drawing attention to the corridor of flags, but he commented adversely about it at the end, using a pejorative term about those who identify with LGBTQ+ groups or causes. Most social media posts are ephemeral, and unless the person posting a video has a very large following, it will be viewed by only a handful of others. This video, most likely, made only the smallest amount of noise inside Goddard's social-media echo chamber, and only for a moment.

The video, nonetheless, came to the attention of a police officer, perhaps because of a complaint from an activist. The police officer's letter confidently asserted that Goddard's comments "would be considered grossly offensive" in contravention of section 127 of the *Communications Act*. The reason the officer gave is that the comments targeted "the LGBTQ community". Consequently, Goddard was required—not asked, but *required*—to arrange a 'voluntary interview'. If he declined to do so, the matter would be referred "for consideration of prosecution". So the 'invitation' was accompanied by a threat.

In fact, the chance that charges would be laid in matters of this kind is not high. Prosecutors' guidelines on prosecuting such matters are written against a background of acknowledging the right of freedom of speech.[12] Those guidelines also require the consent of a senior prosecutor before certain laws, including section 127 of the *Communications Act 2003*, can be used to bring charges—or, if charges are laid, before a prosecution can proceed.

In the 2021 decision of *DPP v Bussetti*, the High Court in England held that, to satisfy the requirements of section 127, the message must have been "not simply offensive but grossly offensive. The fact that the message was in bad taste, even shockingly bad taste, was not enough."[13] In other cases, the courts have made it clear that there is no right not to be offended. As one judge put it in a 1999 decision concerning the arrest of three preachers:

> Free speech includes not only the inoffensive but the irritating, the contentious, the eccentric, the heretical, the unwelcome

---

12 'Communications Offences', *Crown Prosecution Service* (cps.gov.uk/legal-guidance/communications-offences).

13 *DPP v Bussetti* [2021] EWHC 2140 (Admin); see 'Communications Offences', *CPS*.

and the provocative provided it does not tend to provoke violence. Freedom only to speak inoffensively is not worth having.[14]

However, any police involvement in such matters has a chilling effect on freedom of speech. The vast majority of offensive commentary on social media does not attract the use of scarce police resources, and so it is reasonable to ask why some offensive speech receives police attention. Fewer than six percent of offences reported to police led to a suspect being charged or summonsed in 2022-23 in England and Wales.[15] Shoplifting prosecutions have declined to a small fraction of the number of cases prosecuted a decade ago, while reports to the police have increased by a third in the same period.[16] Perhaps the police might have better uses for their time than policing language.

Government: the authority that God has established?

This book is, in essence, about Christians' relationship with governments, and the extent to which, as a consequence of our faith, we should feel a moral obligation to obey the law. Of course, there is usually a legal obligation by definition, but in the complex world of modern legal systems, in which laws regulate so much of personal, social, commercial and community life, even to say we have an obligation to 'obey the law' needs some explanation. There are laws that prohibit conduct on pain of penalty. There are laws that provide a remedy to someone who is affected by what we do or by property we own, in circumstances where we may or may not have been able to prevent the harm claimed. There are regulatory requirements for various organizations where failure to satisfy those requirements on

---

14 Lord Justice Sedley in *Redmond-Bate v DPP* [1999] EWHC Admin 733.

15 Home Office, 'Official Statistics: Crime outcomes in England and Wales 2022 to 2023', *Gov.UK*, 20 July 2023 (www.gov.uk/government/statistics/crime-outcomes-in-england-and-wales-2022-to-2023/crime-outcomes-in-england-and-wales-2022-to-2023).

16 M Dathan, 'Labour: "Shameful neglect" of shoplifting must end', *The Times*, 26 August 2024 (thetimes.com/uk/crime/article/well-end-shameful-neglect-of-shoplifting-by-police-vows-labour-d7wvwjwjj).

time may incur a late fee. If, snowed under with work, I decide that I would rather meet the obligation next month and incur a late fee, am I then 'breaking the law'? There are different kinds of laws, and therefore different kinds of obligations (more on this in chapter 7).

The New Testament certainly indicates that we have an obligation to obey the law. The apostle Paul wrote:

> Let everyone be subject to the governing authorities, for there is no authority except that which God has established. The authorities that exist have been established by God. Consequently, whoever rebels against the authority is rebelling against what God has instituted, and those who do so will bring judgement on themselves. For rulers hold no terror for those who do right, but for those who do wrong. Do you want to be free from fear of the one in authority? Then do what is right and you will be commended. For the one in authority is God's servant for your good. But if you do wrong, be afraid, for rulers do not bear the sword for no reason. They are God's servants, agents of wrath to bring punishment on the wrongdoer. (Rom 13:1–4)

In a similar vein, Peter wrote:

> Submit yourselves for the Lord's sake to every human authority: whether to the emperor, as the supreme authority, or to governors, who are sent by him to punish those who do wrong and to commend those who do right. (1 Pet 2:13–14)

There could be no stronger statements for why Christians are obliged to obey the law and respect the authority of governments. But these passages stand alongside other passages of the Bible that present a different, and perhaps more complex, view of government. We will consider some of these passages throughout the book, especially in chapter 6.

In a sense, every government with laws to regulate society, and a properly functioning legal system to enforce those laws, is carrying out God's work. Even the government of Nazi Germany could be said to come within Paul's endorsement in Romans 13. How could this be, given the Holocaust and the other countless atrocities of this regime?

Consider what it might have been like for a grocery store owner in Munich in the late 1930s. He would have had the benefit of all kinds of laws that would have been, in most respects, quite similar to the laws in Belgium, France or Britain. If he paid for produce that was not delivered, or was delivered unfit for human consumption, he would have had contractual remedies against the supplier. If someone stole from the shop, he could call the police and might have reasonable grounds to think they would prosecute the shoplifter. He could bank the daily proceeds from the shop, assured that the law would support his right to the balance of his account from the bank. In myriad other ways, the laws, and the police that enforced them, would have supported his right to live his life peacefully, to carry on his business, and to provide for his family. His marriage would have been recognized in accordance with German law, and that marriage would have had much the same legal consequences as in any other European nation.

By the time Hitler took his own life in a Berlin bunker in 1945, the law and its legal system had been well and truly subverted to become an instrument of Nazi power. People were imprisoned in concentration camps or deprived of their property; many lost their lives by the exercise of arbitrary powers without reference to established laws.[17] However, such changes only occurred gradually from 1933 onwards. For much of the period of Nazi rule, the small-business owner in Munich would probably think of himself as living in a society governed by law.

Governments are capable of great evil, as the Nazi regime showed; and they carry out that evil at times with the cover of the justice system, which provides a cloak of legitimacy over oppressive acts. However, even governments that routinely violate human rights, or run fraudulent elections to stay in power, or start wars against neighbouring countries—even these governments may still maintain a functioning justice system that looks, to ordinary citizens, much like the law in any other country.

---

17   A Steinweis and R Rachlin (eds), *The Law in Nazi Germany: Ideology, opportunism, and the perversion of justice*, Berghahn Books, 2013.

Brutal governments can make the trains run on time, while governments that have an unequivocal commitment to all human rights may find it difficult to get a functioning railway timetable. A government can be competent without being virtuous, or virtuous without being competent. One of the most important functions of government is to maintain law and order and to enforce the basic rights and obligations of the society. There may be countries where the situation is so chaotic that we can say there is no law at all. To say there is a 'legal system' in a country requires that there be at least some conformity with the minimum requirements of justice. We might call such countries failed states, but few get to the point of complete failure. Even in Chechnya, with its rogue red light, it could be expected that most traffic lights fulfil the function of regulating traffic at intersections.

Living between two kingdoms

As Christians, we are in the world but not of it. Our primary citizenship is in the kingdom of God, but we are also earthly citizens, with obligations to government such as paying taxes (Mark 12:17). All governments, however brutal, undemocratic or oppressive they may be to dissenters, fulfil at least the basic functions of governments, including making and enforcing laws to regulate the society.

Throughout this book, we will discuss more examples of laws that, like the permanently red traffic light, can be weaponized against people of faith or other non-favoured minorities. We will also discuss examples of laws that, in other ways, impact upon the liberties that people of faith have long taken for granted; that reflect a new tendency of governments to regulate churches and Christian organizations in ways that they wouldn't have dreamed of doing a decade or two ago; or that insist that faith-based organizations providing services to the community, such as schools, should operate as if they had almost no faith commitments at all.

These are challenging times for Christians, and for many other 'people of faith'. What does Romans 13 mean, and what do other similar passages mean, in a context where laws may not just regulate the traffic, or enforce contracts, or provide for certainty in land transactions—but instead may require us to act against conscience or may keep us from living out our Christian faith? When might the moral obligation to obey the law be displaced by a moral obligation to disobey it, or at least a moral liberty to do so? How do we navigate a new landscape in which laws are weaponized against followers of Jesus or Christian organizations?

These are, for the most part, very new questions for Christians in these emerging, post-Christian societies. However, they are not new questions for the church around the world or in different periods of history. So, to answer these questions, we need to draw first and foremost on the Bible, but also on the wisdom of the ages and of our brothers and sisters around the world, applying old principles to new contexts.

2

THE DIMINISHING SCOPE FOR RELIGIOUS FREEDOM

*How should Christians respond to an increasingly
threatening legal environment for faith?*

In a great many countries of the world, religious freedom is denied
or severely restricted. Until recently, Western countries (especially Anglophone nations with a Christian heritage) have not been
among them—although going back several centuries, some of these
countries vigorously oppressed people whose religious beliefs were
considered heretical. Jews, as members of a minority faith, also
suffered. Due to virulent anti-Semitism, they were subjected to
pogroms and driven from countries where they had settled.

Some of the intercontinental expansion of both Judaism and
Christianity occurred as people with minority beliefs left European
shores to find religious freedom in North America or beyond. The
colonization of what is now the United States by religious minorities
such as the English Puritans and the French Huguenots is perhaps
the most well-known example. But other parts of the world were
also colonized by people of faith. The South Australian wine industry was established by devout Lutherans who had to leave northern
Germany because of religious persecution. Some died on the long
sea voyage. Pastor Kavel, one of their leaders, wrote about Australia in 1839: "We have found what we have been seeking for many

years—religious liberty—and with all our heart we are desirous of being faithful subjects and useful citizens."[1]

Precisely because so many countries in the Western world were populated by migrants who sought an environment in which they could practice their faith freely, religious freedom has long been a core value of the Western legal tradition. And it still is. If 'freedom of religion' means freedom to attend religious services, then of course it is not under threat. No-one much cares whether I go to church on Sunday mornings any more than they care if I spend my Sunday morning playing video games. I do not expect that to change, because my choice affects no-one else. Therefore, no-one has a reason to stir up a campaign to deprive me of that right. As Professor Stanley Fish once put it, "tolerance is exercised in an inverse proportion to there being anything at stake".[2] That commitment to religious freedom now extends to all faiths in our increasingly multicultural and multi-faith societies.

However, while freedom to gather is not under threat for any religious community, there are growing restrictions in various countries on freedom to practise, or live out, one's faith in daily life. For Muslims, that may be manifested in restrictions on religious dress such as the hijab—something that has occurred particularly in France. For those in the Christian community, where religious forms of dress are typically not central to the expression of faith, restrictions tend to arise from clashes in values with a secular state that is increasingly seeking to drive out dissent on a variety of moral questions. This has been fuelled by a growing and overt hostility to people of faith who hold traditional religious positions on issues such as abortion and homosexual relations. But the attack on people of faith should be understood in a much broader context—one in which both state and corporate power has been pressed into service to stifle dissent on matters that are seen as issues of 'social justice'.

In legal terms, restriction on religious freedom takes many forms. This chapter provides several examples.

1   As recorded in the German Migration Museum, Hahndorf, South Australia.
2   S Fish, 'Almost pragmatism: Richard Posner's Jurisprudence', *University of Chicago Law Review*, 1990, 57(4):1466.

The ever-increasing scope of anti-discrimination laws

The first source of restriction is the expansion of anti-discrimination laws that now produce many more spheres of conflict compared with a generation or two ago. Anti-discrimination laws originated to protect historically disadvantaged groups that had been "subject to widespread denigration and exclusion".[3] The *Civil Rights Act 1964* in the United States is a prominent example. It followed a campaign for social and racial justice, with people of faith such as Dr Martin Luther King at the forefront. It provided a catalyst for the development of similar laws in other countries to prohibit discrimination based on race and gender. Gradually, anti-discrimination law expanded to other fixed characteristics, such as disability.[4]

None of these, other than gender, created problems for people of faith. Gender is an issue for churches that have a theological commitment to a male priesthood or other positions of religious leadership. Male leadership is also traditional in other faiths, such as Orthodox Judaism and Islam. Sensibly, and in accordance with international human-rights conventions, this problem was dealt with in anti-discrimination laws by providing an exemption for those faith communities that chose to rely on it—for example, in relation to religious leaders being male or unmarried. Article 6 of the UN Declaration on the Elimination of all Forms of Intolerance and of Discrimination Based on Religion (1981) specifically provides for the right to "train, appoint, elect or designate by succession appropriate leaders called for by the requirements and standards of any religion or belief".

It is, of course, not unknown for human rights bodies to adopt some rather curious understandings of religious freedom. For example, in 2008, Australia's Human Rights and Equal Opportunities Commission, as it was then known, urged a federal parliamentary Committee to remove the exemption in the *Sex Discrimination Act 1984* that applies to priests and other religious leaders. The

---

3   TM Scanlon, *Moral Dimensions*, Harvard University Press, 2008, p 74.
4   N Rees et al., *Australian Anti-Discrimination Law: Text, Cases and Materials*, Federation Press, 2008, p 16ff.

Commission suggested replacing the exemption with a transitional exemption that would expire after three years unless re-enacted.[5] It argued that the existing law "does not provide support for women of faith who are promoting gender equality within their religious body". In effect, it was proposed that the Australian government should interfere in the life of autonomous and voluntary religious organizations such as the Catholic Church—organizations that operate across the world—by taking sides on a theological question.

Even those who have great sympathy with movements for female ordination might recognize the hubris and overreach of such a proposition. Government control of churches was the norm in the communist countries of Eastern Europe, and this is the position today in many nations around the world. But Western democracies have until now recognized that it is not the role of government to dictate to religious organizations who should be eligible for positions of leadership.

While such radical ideas about using the law to coerce churches is generally confined to the ivory tower, increasingly anti-discrimination laws have presented other conflicts for people of faith. This is because, in some jurisdictions at least, there has been a massive expansion of the scope of such laws to cover 'protected attributes'. A 'protected attribute' is a characteristic of a person that is covered by an anti-discrimination law. This used to cover inherent attributes such as race or gender, or unchosen states such as living with a disability. But the notion has evolved to include people's social and moral choices, such as whether to get married, or whether to engage in sexual conduct outside of marriage.

Take two Australian states: at time of writing, there are 22 different grounds on which someone can make a complaint about discrimination in Tasmania, and 21 in Victoria. In both jurisdictions, "lawful sexual conduct" is now a protected attribute. Another is "marital status"; in Tasmania, "relationship status" is protected. The

---

5   Human Rights and Equal Opportunities Commission, 'Inquiry into the effectiveness of the Sex Discrimination Act 1984 (Cth) in eliminating discrimination and promoting gender equality, September 2008', *Australian Human Rights Commission*, 1 September 2008, p 166.

exemptions for religious organizations in both states are very limited.

To illustrate the potential harm of this expansion of anti-discrimination law, we may ask: could a church lawfully dismiss a paid youth worker who performs religious and pastoral duties and who, it has been discovered, has been 'sleeping around' and has had multiple sexual partners within a short period of time? Such activity is lawful. But any church that believes and follows the Bible would consider this behaviour to be inconsistent with their values and standards. Indeed, this view would almost certainly be common to Christianity, Judaism and Islam. In a state without religious exemptions, however, the dismissal of the youth worker could lead to a claim of discrimination on the basis of "lawful sexual conduct".

The law in Queensland offers another example of almost irreconcilable conflicts between faith and anti-discrimination law. Amendments to the anti-discrimination law that came into effect in August 2024 prohibit discrimination on the basis of "sex work activity".[6] Sex work is defined as "the provision by an adult person of the following services for payment or reward—

i)   services that involve the person participating in a sexual activity with another person;
ii) services that involve the use or display of the person's body for the sexual arousal or gratification of another person".

The Queensland Human Rights Commission's information page makes it clear that this includes actors in pornographic films and those creating online content.[7] Consider a situation where a female teacher at a school is discovered to be creating such content—making money in her spare time by displaying her body online to people who are willing to pay. Her conduct comes to the attention of the school leadership after photographs of her are widely disseminated among the student body. It is hard to imagine that a principal of a state school would be any happier about this situation than the principal of a Christian school. Yet the principal of the state school

---

6   *Anti-Discrimination Act 1991* (Qld), s 7(1).
7   Queensland Human Rights Commission, 'Sex work activity', QHRC website, 2 August 2024 (qhrc.qld.gov.au/your-rights/discrimination-law/sex-work-activity).

might have difficulty dismissing the teacher, given that she is engaging in lawful "sex work activity" according to the legislation.

The Christian school might not be in a much better position. The legislation allows for faith-based schools to discriminate in relation to conduct *if* the person openly acts in a way that the person knows (or ought reasonably to know) is contrary to the employer's religious beliefs. But this only applies if they do so in the course of their work, or in something connected with their work.[8] The question would arise: is this teacher's "sex work activity" connected with her work at the school?

The most obvious conflict between religious freedom and anti-discrimination laws is, at least potentially, in relation to homosexual relationships. The position of faith communities on this is often misunderstood. Apart from the marriage issue, most faith communities support anti-discrimination laws to protect gay, lesbian and bisexual people. The Catechism of the Catholic Church provides:

> The number of men and women who have deep-seated homosexual tendencies is not negligible ... They must be accepted with respect, compassion, and sensitivity. Every sign of unjust discrimination in their regard should be avoided.[9]

Faith communities have, nonetheless, been mostly opposed to changes in such a fundamental institution as marriage. Yet this also has been misunderstood. The best reasons for this opposition are thoughtful and nuanced, based not in bigotry or in any kind of 'phobia', but in careful and faithful readings of the Bible. Moreover, there would have been similar opposition to the legalization of heterosexual polygamy or, more generally, polyamorous relationships.

Nonetheless, issues do arise around whether those living in homosexual relationships are eligible for leadership position in religious communities. Some churches have sought to forge a compromise between different viewpoints, while others have remained firmly committed to traditional doctrines and understandings of biblical

8 *Anti-Discrimination Act 1991* (Qld), s 25(3).
9 The Catechism of the Catholic Church, second edn, Libreria Editrice Vaticana, 1994, paragraph 2358.

teaching. Those who take a conservative theological position on this are particularly likely to be in conflict with anti-discrimination law unless they can rely on an exemption.

The war on religious exemptions

Traditionally, anti-discrimination laws have dealt with the clash of conflicting rights and freedoms by crafting exemptions for certain contexts. One such context is to allow faith-based organizations and their leaders to maintain their beliefs, values and ethos.

The *Equality Act 2010* in Britain provides an illustration. Under schedule 23 of the Act, a religious organization (other than one whose sole or main purpose is commercial) can limit membership and participation in its activities without contravening the Act.[10] This exemption applies where the restriction on the basis of belief is central to the organization's purpose, or to avoid causing offence to members of that religion or belief. Similar exemptions relate to sexual orientation, provided a restriction is necessary to comply with the doctrine of the religion or because of the strongly held religious convictions of many adherents. In a multicultural society, provisions like this will be necessary for religious organizations, and particularly for minority religious groups, to maintain their beliefs and values.

While most jurisdictions contain exemptions of this kind, activists for 'equality' have unleashed a sustained attack on such exemptions, particularly where they are seen to restrict 'rights' on the basis of a person's sexual orientation or gender identity. In the face of such attacks, exemptions were largely abolished in Victoria in 2021;[11] there are also very limited exemptions in Tasmania.

This campaign to remove exemptions reflects a particular view of the State's role in regulating churches and other religious organizations—a much more expansive view than has ever been known in the past. Michael McConnell, a former academic lawyer and US federal judge, explains that in a previous era, state neutrality, tolerance

10 *Equality Act 2010*, schedule 23, paragraph 2.
11 *Equal Opportunity (Religious Exceptions) Amendment Act 2021* (Vic).

and the guarantee of equality before the law meant, fundamentally, that the government would not take sides in religious and philosophical disputes among the people. But now, "there is a widespread sense not only that the government should be neutral, tolerant and egalitarian, but so should all of us, and so should our private associations".[12] On this view, a religious belief is not necessarily a sufficient justification for discrimination, even in relation to the staffing of a religious organization such as a Christian school.

Underlying this campaign against exemptions are two beliefs that are stated with a dogmatism that is as powerful and rigid as any belief system of religious groups. First, there is a belief that all limitations on who is eligible to apply for particular jobs should be abolished or severely restricted in the name of one idea of 'equality', even if the person could apply for the great majority of other jobs for which he or she is qualified. This position involves taking a very restrictive approach to 'genuine occupational requirements' as a ground for exceptions to anti-discrimination laws.

But there is a second fundamentalist aspect of the campaign against exemptions. It arises from the belief that the only human rights that should be given any real significance are *individual* rights, not *group* rights. This can lead advocates to disregard the claims of communities that would justify a right of choosing staff who will enhance the cohesion and identity of a religious or cultural organization. In other words, the rights of communities are to be sacrificed on the altar of the rights of the individual.

Charity law and public benefit

Another reason why religious freedom has become constrained relates to developments in the regulation of charities. In common-law countries, which include England, Wales, Australia and New Zealand, an organization will be considered 'charitable' if it advances religion. To say that an organization is charitable does not mean that

12   M McConnell, 'Why is religious freedom the first freedom?', *Cardozo Law Review*, 2000, 21:1243.

taxpayer donations to it are tax-deductible; that depends on laws in each country. However, it typically means that the organization is exempt from tax on its income, and it may have other benefits.

While most religious organizations will be considered charitable, there is also a requirement that they be for the 'public benefit'. At common law, this was satisfied as long as any member of the public could attend. A closed and contemplative order of nuns, for example, was held not be charitable because the law does not view such a religious order as conferring a public benefit.[13]

In various countries, the regulation of charities has been tightened considerably in recent years, and the test of public benefit has become more stringent as a result of legislation. For example, the *Charities Act 2011* of England and Wales provides that there is no presumption that a category of organization, such as one to advance religion, is for the public benefit. To satisfy the test, the purposes of the organization must be beneficial, and any detriment or harm that results from the purpose must not outweigh the benefit. Importantly, equality legislation is now factored into the assessment of public benefit. So, for example, in *Catholic Care (Diocese of Leeds) v Charity Commission*, Briggs J stated:

> An organization which proposes to fulfil a purpose for the public benefit will only qualify as a charity if, taking into account any disbenefit arising from its modus operandi, its activities none the less yield a net public benefit ... Thus, a charity which proposed to apply differential treatment on grounds of sexual orientation otherwise than as a proportionate means of achieving a legitimate aim might thereby fail to achieve charitable status (or lose it, if it sought to pursue such activities by amendment of its objects).[14]

As a consequence of judicial decisions on this issue, all Catholic adoption agencies in England and Wales have either severed their connections to the Church or closed, although one has been

13 *Gilmour v Coats* [1949] AC 426 (House of Lords).
14 *Catholic Care (Diocese of Leeds) v Charity Commission* [2012] 4 All ER 1041 at 97.

permitted to remain in Scotland while restricting access to the service to heterosexual married couples.[15]

Similar issues have arisen in New Zealand. An organization called Family First is engaged in public advocacy on a broad range of family issues in New Zealand. It is informed by a religious perspective, and holds a traditional view of marriage. In 2013, the Charities Board decided it should be stripped of its charitable status because its main purpose was to promote points of view about family life that included the defence of traditional marriage. This was seen to be a non-charitable political purpose that did not have a public benefit. The High Court ordered the Charities Board to reconsider its decision, but the same outcome was reached in August 2017.

This decision to deregister the charity was ultimately upheld by the Supreme Court of New Zealand.[16] The Supreme Court considered that Family First's publications were not for the advancement of education because their purpose was to advocate for, or persuade people to, Family First's point of view. On this logic, no think tank that seeks to persuade people to its point of view could be charitable.

Furthermore, the Supreme Court said Family First's purposes were not self-evidently beneficial because they were discriminatory:

> Family First's purposes are themselves discriminatory. As is made clear in its Principles on Family, Family First affirms the traditional man/woman family to be "the natural family"; that this natural family "cannot change into some new shape" or be "re-defined by social engineering"; and that the marital union is "the authentic sexual bond, the only one open to the natural and responsible creation of new life". As the High Court Judge noted, Family First advocates for measures to prefer the traditional family and disadvantage others, such as amending tax and welfare law to eliminate disincentives to marriage. It also advocates a fault-based law for dissolution of a marriage, placing the weight of the law on the side of the spouse resisting dissolution.

15 St Margaret's Child and Family Services, Glasgow. See 'Scottish Catholic agency will not consider same-sex adopters', *Catholic Courier*, 2 March 2014 (catholiccourier. com/articles/scottish-catholic-agency-will-not-consider-same-sex-adopters).
16 *Attorney-General v Family First New Zealand* [2022] NZSC 80.

None of this is self-evidently beneficial. Nor do we consider that Family First can establish benefit.[17]

The Court considered that "a purpose to discriminate (or a purpose that includes discriminatory elements) is not compatible with a charitable purpose".[18]

One commentator has observed:

> The Supreme Court decision in Family First has the potential to be used arbitrarily as a weapon against any charity that happens to express a view any given decisionmaker does not agree with. If Family First can be deregistered for engaging in the democratic process, any charity can.[19]

The redefinition of child abuse and neglect

Systems that have been established for safeguarding children can be weaponized to express disapproval of beliefs or to require certain kinds of behaviour that could well be damaging to children. This was the experience of one English mother, Carrie, whose 14-year-old daughter decided she was not sure whether she was a girl. Like so many teenage girls who identify as transgender or non-binary, she went to an academically high-performing school. Without the mother's knowledge or consent, the school began to treat the girl as male—notwithstanding that it was an all-girls school! When the mother found out and did not accept the school's treatment of her daughter, she came to be regarded as a 'safeguarding risk', and the school reported her to social services three times. The ordeal went on for four years.[20]

---

17 *Attorney-General v Family First New Zealand* at paragraphs 137–138.
18 *Attorney-General v Family First New Zealand* at paragraph 139.
19 S Barker, 'The Supreme Court decision in Family First—a gift to the forces of authoritarianism?', *LinkedIn*, 5 July 2022 (linkedin.com/pulse/supreme-court-decision-family-first-gift-forces-susan-barker).
20 A Hurynag, 'Mother battles schools adopting child's preferred gender "without consent"', *Sky News*, 19 December 2023 (news.sky.com/story/mother-battles-schools-adopting-childs-preferred-gender-without-consent-13034212).

The view that it is child abuse *not* to agree that your teenage daughter is 'really' a boy is not an isolated one. In its first issue in 2024, the prestigious American journal *Pediatrics* published a paper in which three authors, two of whom are clinicians at Seattle Children's Hospital, argued that withholding puberty blockers or cross-sex hormones from trans-identifying children or young people amounts to medical neglect or emotional abuse.[21]

The redefinition of ideas of child abuse and neglect is not specifically a problem of religious freedom. Many parents could, like Carrie, find themselves reported to child-protection authorities for refusing to go along with their daughter's beliefs about 'being born in the wrong body', whether or not they also hold religious beliefs. However, such laws may specifically be targeted against people of faith. This was the experience of Glawdys Leger, a high-school teacher who was dismissed from a Church of England School because she refused to teach Year 7 and 8 pupils certain required materials concerning sexualities and gender identities. She told a class that she did not believe in transgender ideology, and that Christians believe sex outside of heterosexual marriage is sinful. She was dismissed for gross misconduct, with her employer claiming she represented a risk to the "emotional well-being of children". She was then referred to the Teaching Regulation Agency, which made an adverse finding against her but stopped short of banning her from the teaching profession for life.[22]

Other teachers have not been so fortunate. For example, Kevin Lister, a teacher in Swindon, was dismissed from his teaching

---

21 E Georges et al., 'Prohibition of gender-affirming care as a form of child maltreatment: Reframing the discussion', *Pediatrics*, January 2024, 153(1):e2023064292 (doi.org/10.1542/peds.2023-064292).

22 Teaching Regulation Agency, 20 December 2023; S Caldwell, 'Catholic teacher guilty of professional misconduct after refusing to indoctrinate children in extremist ideology', *Catholic Herald*, 21 December 2023 (catholicherald.co.uk/catholic-teacher-guilty-of-professional-misconduct-after-refusing-to-indoctrinate-children-in-extremist-ideology); W Jones, 'Teacher found guilty of gross misconduct and branded a "safeguarding risk" for sharing Christian beliefs on gender and marriage in Church of England school', *The Daily Sceptic*, 21 December 2023 (dailysceptic.org/2023/12/21/teacher-found-guilty-of-gross-misconduct-and-branded-a-safeguarding-risk-for-sharing-christian-beliefs-on-gender-and-marriage-in-church-of-england-school).

position and then barred from teaching for life in December 2023 for refusing to go along with a 17-year-old girl's wish to be called a boy, and for warning her of the risks of embarking on irreversible cross-sex hormone treatment.[23] He is appealing the ban.

Health regulation and the demise of conscientious objection

Article 18 of the *International Covenant on Civil and Political Rights*, the most important human-rights covenant in the world, provides that "everyone shall have the right to freedom of thought, conscience and religion". Traditionally, health care has been an area where a doctor or nurse's freedom of conscience has been respected. Abortion laws, for example, typically provide that health professionals are not mandated to participate in a non-emergency abortion procedure. The *Abortion Act 1967* in Britain offers an example. Section 4 provides:

> Subject to subsection (2) of this section, no person shall be under any duty, whether by contract or by any statutory or other legal requirement, to participate in any treatment authorised by this Act to which he has a conscientious objection …
>
> (2) Nothing in subsection (1) of this section shall affect any duty to participate in treatment which is necessary to save the life or to prevent grave permanent injury to the physical or mental health of a pregnant woman.

However, the scope for conscientious objection has been narrowed in some jurisdictions. Doctors may be required either to refer the patient to someone who has no such objection,[24] or to provide the patient with contact details of such a person.[25] This can be a source of attack on Christian doctors who feel unable to cooperate

---

23   B Smith, 'Teacher is banned for "misgendering" pupil'", *The Telegraph*, 23 December 2023 (telegraph.co.uk/news/2023/12/23/teacher-is-banned-for-misgendering-pupil).

24   See, for example, *Termination of Pregnancy Act 2018*, s 8 (Qld).

25   See, for example, New Zealand: R Ahdar, 'Conscientious objection to abortion revisited', *Oxford Journal of Law and Religion*, 7 March 2022 (doi.org/10.1093/ojlr/rwac006).

in any way with the abortion process. In Victoria, for example, the law requires doctors to refer patients inquiring for an abortion to another doctor, even if the doctor has a conscientious objection to making such a referral.[26] This provision was passed despite the opposition of the Australian Medical Association.[27]

The case of Dr Mark Hobart in Victoria is illustrative of the need for better protection of freedom of conscience. A couple asked Dr Hobart, a GP, to refer them to an abortion practitioner. The woman was 19 weeks' pregnant at the time. The reason for the request was that during a routine ultrasound, they had discovered that the baby was a girl. As Dr Hobart understood it, the requested abortion was purely for sex-selection purposes. The doctor refused to refer, but the abortion was carried out one week later. The Medical Board of Victoria decided to investigate his refusal to refer, resulting in a formal caution in 2013 after an investigation lasting eight months.[28]

The Australian Human Rights Commission has argued strongly against the expansion of any right to conscientious objection beyond existing concessions, using Victoria's requirement that doctors refer to another doctor as an example of an appropriate limitation on this human right.[29] One consequence of the very limited protection for conscientious objection in Australia is that while doctors and nurses are typically given freedom to opt out of providing an abortion or performing euthanasia, conscientious objection is typically not extended to fertility specialists who might object to the provision of IVF services to single women or same-sex couples.

In New Zealand, employers even have the right to dismiss staff who have a conscientious objection to participating in abortions if their refusal to be involved "would unreasonably disrupt the

26   *Abortion Law Reform Act 2008* (Vic).
27   F Brennan, 'The place of the religious viewpoint in shaping law and policy in a pluralistic democratic society: a case study on rights and conscience'. Paper given at Values and Public Policy Conference: Fairness, Diversity and Social Change, Centre for Public Policy, University of Melbourne, 26 February 2009.
28   Dr Hobart's own account is available in a submission to the Queensland Parliament.
29   Australian Human Rights Commission, 'Submission to the Select Committee on the Exposure Draft of the Marriage Amendment (Same-Sex Marriage) Bill', Australian Human Rights Commission website, 18 January 2017 at pp 21ff.

employer's provision of health services".[30] The High Court of New Zealand has held that this provision does not discriminate against people on the basis of their religious beliefs because people may also object to abortion on grounds other than religious faith. Even if the provision contravened the right of people to be free from discrimination on the basis of religion, said the judge, the law's limits on the right to conscientious objection can be "demonstrably justified in free and democratic society" because of the overriding need to protect women's human right to access abortions.[31]

Christian organizations as agents of the State

A final reason for the decline in religious freedom in Western societies is the role of Christian organizations in providing welfare programs.

In many countries, welfare organizations associated with churches now receive most of their funding from governments. This money is to provide services to the population on a very large scale that governments would otherwise have to provide themselves. The details of this vary from one country to another, but the kinds of services that Christian welfare organizations provide include aged care, support for the homeless, other poverty-relief programs, treatment programs for alcohol, drug or gambling addiction, employment services, family support programs, foster care, adolescent residential care services, hospitals, and schools. Of course, it is not only Christian organizations that are funded in this way. Such non-government organizations (NGOs) are a subset of a larger group of not-for-profit or 'third sector' organizations that receive government funds to deliver social services.

From the government's point of view, this outsourcing of service delivery to non-profit organizations has numerous benefits, apart from the quality and efficiency of services delivered. Outsourcing to such NGOs avoids the costs to government of acquiring and

---

30 *Abortion Regulation Act 2020*, s 15(2).
31 *New Zealand Health Professionals Alliance Incorporated v Attorney-General* [2021] NZHC 2510.

maintaining infrastructure and staff for the management and delivery of those services.

Typically, not-for-profit organizations bid for government contracts to deliver services, and those contracts have a limited shelf-life. The government is, of course, under no obligation to renew a contract; it may decide to re-price the contract, or to impose additional obligations on the NGO without increased funding, making continuation of the service uneconomic. That leaves the NGO with the obligation to pay for redundancies if staff cannot be offered suitable work elsewhere in the organization. It may also be left with the cost of renting or maintaining buildings that are no longer needed.

But government funding comes with an additional cost. The argument is made that if the government is providing almost all the funding for an organization—or even a substantial majority of it—then the organization should reflect governmental values concerning equity, diversity and inclusion. That may make it very difficult for the faith-based organization to maintain its Christian identity and ethos. The level of government funding involved can also make it difficult to argue that religious exemptions in anti-discrimination laws should apply to that organization.

Churches and other Christian ministries faced with these pressures therefore have something of a dilemma. On the one hand, local congregations have largely outsourced their responsibilities to care for the poor and needy in a community to these large professional organizations that provide these services in the name of Christ. On the other hand, these services are increasingly limited in their capacity to be overt about their Christian motivation and mission, or in their ability to prefer active Christians for employment. Indeed, in some large organizations, only a minority of staff are committed to the Christian faith. These organizations are, in essence, agents of the State, and eventually the pressures to be entirely secular are likely to be overwhelming.

3

THE WEAPONIZATION OF LAWS

How is law being weaponized against people of faith?

It would be a complete misunderstanding of the laws discussed in chapter 2 to think that they are designed to diminish religious freedom, even though they will sometimes have this effect. Anti-discrimination laws, for example, did not originate out of a concern to secularize the society or to diminish the freedom of people of faith to live differently from other groups in the community. On the contrary, the original motivation was to promote equality of opportunity and treatment in areas such as employment and education. It is only as the scope of anti-discrimination laws has expanded, and exemptions to support freedom of religion and association have been curtailed, that anti-discrimination laws have become a potential source of attack on people of faith.

Although some laws that may restrict religious freedom may not be intended to achieve that purpose, they can be weaponized in various ways against people of faith in pursuit of socio-political objectives. Much depends on how they are implemented. Police, courts and tribunals can be co-opted as means through which wars on ideas can be waged if the conditions for doing so are right. When this happens, people are forced to pay a price to defend those ideas, irrespective of the outcome of the complaint. Such strategies are undoubtedly successful. People self-censor rather than putting themselves at risk of having the police knock at the door, or being summoned by the HR team at work to answer a complaint.

In this chapter, we will consider various ways in which the law is being weaponized against Christians.

Hate speech

One way in which laws and complaints procedures can be weaponized is by reference to hated viewpoints, which are characterized as being 'hate speech'. It has become very common in recent years to hear viewpoints described this way in the press, on television or in social media. The UN Strategy and Plan of Action on Hate Speech defines hate speech as "any kind of communication in speech, writing or behaviour, that attacks or uses pejorative or discriminatory language with reference to a person or a group on the basis of who they are, in other words, based on their religion, ethnicity, nationality, race, colour, descent, gender or other identity factor".[1] The UN seeks to combat hate speech wherever speech supports xenophobia, racism, intolerance, violent misogyny, anti-Semitism and anti-Muslim hatred around the world.

The concern about hate speech, rightly understood, is entirely valid. Very often, hate speech lays the foundation for violence against the minority groups that are its target. In the conflicts between Israel and the Palestinians, for example, calls to drive out the Jews entirely from the land of Israel are commonly part of the rhetoric of extremist religious leaders and political activists. Language of that kind is a call to violence against Jews in Israel, to be sure, and may incite violence against Jews in other places. Laws that prohibit incitement to violence are necessary in a multicultural society that seeks to keep the peace—not only between Muslims and Jews, but between other groups or races who may have a long history of conflict. It is also necessary to prohibit incitement of hatred or violence against people on the basis of other characteristics, such as the colour of their skin or a known sexual orientation.

---

1   United Nations, 'The UN Strategy and Plan of Action on Hate Speech', United Nations website (un.org/en/hate-speech/un-strategy-and-plan-of-action-on-hate-speech).

Hateful points of view

While hate speech laws fulfil an important role as a response to speech that may incite others to violence or abuse, they have evolved over time, in some jurisdictions and contexts, into weapons of ideological conflict. That is, the idea of 'hate speech' has metamorphosed in certain places from 'speech motivated by hate' or 'intended to inspire hate', to apply to any speech expressing a view that the listener hates, and which is perceived to be harmful to others. In this way, the prohibition on hate speech has been extended to ideas that are perceived to be offensive or harmful to certain vulnerable groups of people. These ideas have travelled from the elite universities of the United States to other Anglophone countries and beyond.

This is the basis of what is called 'cancel culture'. It is a major reason why laws that were seen as necessary to protect public safety and community harmony have been turned into weapons to be used in battles of ideas and beliefs. So, the argument goes, if an idea might cause 'emotional harm' to another, or if it harms the 'dignity' of a person or group, it is not legitimate, and ought not be protected by notions of free speech. This viewpoint has been manifested in an argument that some issues—such as whether same-sex couples should be allowed to marry—should not even be debated publicly, because the debate itself will cause emotional harm to those whose lives are the subject of that debate.

This metamorphosis has been facilitated by law enforcement redefining hate speech in a way that relies upon the complainant's perception of what has motivated the speech being complained about. For example, the inspectorate of police services in England and Wales defined a 'hate incident' in a 2018 publication as one "perceived by the victim, or any other person, to be motivated by hostility or prejudice towards someone based on a personal characteristic".[2] These "personal characteristics" are said to include "race or ethnicity", "religions or beliefs", "sexual orientation", "disability" or "transgender identity".

2   *Understanding the Difference: The Initial Police Response to Hate Crime*, July 2018, p 7 (hmicfrs.justiceinspectorates.gov.uk/publications/understanding-the-difference-the-initial-police-response-to-hate-crime).

In this definition, the perception of hostility or prejudice need not be a reasonable one. In a polarized society, in which social media algorithms put a premium on outrage, it will not be uncommon for a listener or reader to attribute motives based on hostility or prejudice, rather than, say, different beliefs or worldviews. The definition of a hate incident used by the English inspectorate of police services does not even require that the person with the relevant personal characteristic perceives someone's words or conduct to be motivated by hate. It is enough for someone else, someone not personally affected, to perceive that hate provided the motivation. In this way, reporting an alleged 'hate crime' to the police can become a tool of activism for those who are offended on behalf of others.

The criminalization of offensive ideas

Hate speech may be the basis for a criminal offence. In April 2021, the Finnish Prosecutor-General brought three criminal charges against a former government minister, Dr Päivi Räsänen, because of views she expressed on human sexuality. The investigation of her for a hate-speech crime arose initially from a post she made on X (then Twitter) criticizing the leadership of her denomination, the Evangelical Lutheran Church of Finland, for its official partnership with the 'Pride 2019' event. She was also prosecuted for comments she made in a radio debate, and for a church pamphlet she wrote with a bishop concerning the Church's teaching on homosexuality as long ago as 2004. The bishop, the Rev Dr Jujana Pohjola, was also charged in relation to the pamphlet. The charges related to "ethnic agitation", which carries a maximum penalty of two years imprisonment. However, the basis of these charges was nothing more than that two prominent people had expressed hated ideas publicly.

Räsänen and Pohjola were eventually acquitted of these charges, and the prosecutor's initial appeal against the decision was dismissed. But at time of writing, the prosecutor has taken a further appeal to Finland's highest court—a clear indication of his commitment to using the criminal law as a weapon against hated ideas.[3]

Elsewhere, bills aimed at strengthening laws on hate speech have proved very controversial, not least because of their potential impact on freedom of speech. This was the case, for example, in Scotland, where the Hate Crimes and Public Order (Scotland) Bill 2020 was widely perceived as threatening freedom of speech—including speech in the privacy of one's home. If a communication of "threatening or abusive material" related to a group characterized by age, disability, religion, sexual orientation or transgender identity, it could be considered an offence if it was deemed "likely" that hatred would be stirred up against such a group (whether or not anyone did react with hatred).[4] The Bill even contained a section creating legal liability for those involved in the public performance of a play that was likely to stir up hatred.[5]

Prior to enactment in 2021, the Bill was substantially revised to provide that speech is only criminal where it is *intended* to stir up hatred.[6] Proving beyond reasonable doubt that there is intent to cause a reaction in someone else will be very difficult. Other provisions were also added to protect freedom of speech. But the legislation, as finally enacted, also includes a curious bias: it explicitly allows speech that shows "antipathy, dislike, ridicule or insult" for religion, but not for any other protected category.

While the legislation has continued to cause controversy, it is not likely to be the attack on free speech that some may have feared. It has long been an offence to stir up racial hatred. However, there is a difference between criminalizing speech that allegedly may stir up hatred based upon the colour of one's skin and speaking in a critical way about religion or transgender identification. The latter two categories involve ideas and beliefs, not immutable characteristics.

The most likely impact of hate-crime laws such as those in

3   ADF International, 'Bible-tweet case to be heard at Finnish Supreme Court', ADF International website, 19 April 2024 (adfinternational.org/news/bible-tweet-case-to-be-heard-at-finnish-supreme-court).

4   *Hate Crimes and Public Order (Scotland) Bill 2020*, s 3(2).

5   *Hate Crimes and Public Order (Scotland) Bill 2020*, s 4.

6   *Hate Crimes and Public Order (Scotland) Act 2021*, s 4(2)(b).

Scotland will be to tie the police up in paperwork responding to complaints about other people's ideas and beliefs on these matters. In the first week of the operation of the law, police received more than 8,000 complaints—in a country of about 5.5 million, smaller than a great many cities around the world.[7] The Chairman of the Scottish Police Federation told the BBC that police were overwhelmed, and that people had "weaponized" the law to pursue personal and political vendettas. This illustrates how such laws can be misused in battles about ideas. The necessity at least to consider all such complaints and to document decision-making detracts from the police's ability to investigate other crimes or alleged assaults, a great many of which are either not investigated or receive only a cursory investigation by over-stretched police forces.

Anti-vilification laws

Other hate-speech laws provide civil remedies, such as orders for compensation or requirements to remove offensive materials from the internet. Some such laws make it unlawful to offend another person on the basis of a particular characteristic. An example is section 18C of the *Racial Discrimination Act 1975*, a federal law in Australia. It provides:

> It is unlawful for a person to do an act, otherwise than in private, if:
>> (a) the act is reasonably likely, in all the circumstances, to offend, insult, humiliate or intimidate another person or a group of people; and
>> (b) the act is done because of the race, colour or national or ethnic origin of the other person or of some or all of the people in the group.

An unlawful act of this kind can be the basis of a complaint to the Australian Human Rights Commission. An 'act' includes speech, but

---

7   C Hymas, 'Hate crime complaints to Scottish police set to outnumber total for all other offences', *The Telegraph*, 9 April 2024 (telegraph.co.uk/news/2024/04/08/police-scotland-cannot-cope-deluge-hate-crime-reports).

the law protects anything said or done reasonably and in good faith for any genuine academic, artistic or scientific purpose or another purpose deemed to be in the public interest.[8]

Anti-vilification laws may also apply to religious belief, sexual orientation or gender identity, and it is in such contexts that the law can be weaponized against religious ideas. In Australia, perhaps the most well-known example of a broad hate speech law is section 17 of the *Anti-Discrimination Act 1998* in Tasmania. This makes it unlawful for a person to "engage in any conduct which offends, humiliates, intimidates, insults or ridicules another person" based on various attributes, including race, age, sexual orientation, lawful sexual activity, gender, gender identity, intersex, marital status, relationship status, pregnancy, breastfeeding, parental status or family responsibilities. The qualifier here is that the conduct (which includes speech) must have occurred in circumstances in which a reasonable person, having regard to all the circumstances, would have anticipated that the other person would be offended, humiliated, intimidated, insulted or ridiculed. The remedy is a civil one: a person can be sued for breaching the law and be liable to pay damages.

This section was used to bring a complaint against Julian Porteous, the Catholic Archbishop of Hobart. In the context of a national debate on whether to legalize same-sex marriage, he distributed a booklet to parents of children in Catholic schools. The booklet was put out by the Australian Catholic Bishops Conference defending its traditional view of marriage. Though the Bishops expressed their view in a very moderate and reasoned way, they, along with Archbishop Porteous, were required to answer the complaint. The basis was only that the complainant had been offended by ideas either expressed in the publication or said to be implied in the Church's defence of a traditional view of marriage as between a man and a woman. The complainant was a candidate for a political party.[9]

What is remarkable about this case is not that it was brought, for

8   *Racial Discrimination Act 1975*, s 18D.
9   See, for example, 'Anti-gay marriage book offends: campaigner', *9 News*, 28 September 2015 (9news.com.au/national/anti-gay-marriage-booklet-sparks-complaint/15edd461-f97c-4650-bf22-aa9286e8d03d).

anyone is entitled to use legal processes to address their grievances. Rather, what is troubling is that it was accepted by the Anti-Discrimination Commissioner, who saw it as a potentially valid complaint under the legislation.[10] Eventually the complaint was dropped, but not before the Archbishop had had to utilize his time and resources defending a claim that should have been immediately rejected on the ground that the complaint was unreasonable, given Australia's commitment to freedom of religion and speech.

This is not an isolated incident. In September 2020, a member of the Federal Parliament, Senator Claire Chandler, received a letter from the Tasmanian Equal Opportunity Commission. The Anti-Discrimination Commissioner summoned her to attend a mediation over an email she had sent to a constituent. In this letter, and a related article, she had expressed the view that women's sports changing rooms and toilets were designed for those of the female sex and should remain that way.[11]

The Commissioner found that the Senator's view was "problematic" and that a member of the LGBTQ+ community might reasonably be humiliated, intimidated, offended and insulted. The Commissioner also expressed her personal view that it may no longer be necessary to have separate toilets based on sex.[12] As a public official exercising her duty to administer an anti-discrimination law fairly, it might be thought that she should not express a view on such policy issues. Moreover, the complainant did not identify as transgender. Like the complaint against Archbishop Porteous, eventually the complaint was withdrawn. It costs nothing to make a complaint, and to do so involves little more than filling in a simple form; but it can take much effort to respond to a complaint of this kind.

10 For an account, see 'Anti-discrimination commissioner notifies archbishop of possible breach of the law' in *The Catholic Weekly*, 13 November 2015 (catholicweekly. com.au/anti-discrimination-commissioner-reportedly-finds-archbishop-julian-porteous-in-possible-breach-of-act).

11 C Uhlmann, 'When freedom of speech is in transition', *Sydney Morning Herald*, 30 September 2020 (smh.com.au/national/when-freedom-of-speech-is-in-transition-20200929-p5608l.html).

12 'Senator in hot water for "humiliating" transgender changeroom remarks', *Mercury*, 5 September 2020.

While the Tasmanian law on causing offence is widest in scope, it is one among many. A section of Australia's federal Criminal Code makes it an offence to use a telephone, send a text message, use the internet or use social media to convey a message that "reasonable persons would regard as being, in all the circumstances ... offensive".[13] There is an equivalent provision in relation to postal services,[14] although cases are unlikely to be brought to court unless they reach a high threshold of seriousness.[15]

In Britain, laws that prohibit causing offence can be invoked to punish the expression of ideas that complainants consider hateful. For example, in March 2023, a woman who was in the female psychiatric ward of a hospital in Derbyshire was formally summoned by police after another woman in the ward who identified as 'non-binary' overheard a discussion with the nurse about whether that person was still a woman notwithstanding her non-binary identification. This was said to be a public order offence because the words were highly offensive.[16] What it means to identify as 'non-binary' in the context of admission to single-sex facilities ought reasonably to be a matter for discussion and debate, given that gender identity is so often said to displace biological sex. In acting on complaints about such issues in a way that intimidates people from expressing their views on one side of that argument, the police are effectively co-opted to advance highly contentious socio-political objectives.

It is not only laws against causing offence that may be weaponized to support certain agendas and causes. For example, section 4A

13 *Criminal Code Act 1995*, section 474.17. Whether something is offensive is judged by "the standards of morality, decency and propriety generally accepted by reasonable adults; the literary, artistic or educational merit (if any) of the material; and the general character of the material (including whether it is of a medical, legal or scientific character)" (s 473(4)).

14 *Criminal Code Act 1995*, s 471(12).

15 In Australian federal law, the notion of causing offence has been strictly interpreted by the High Court: *Monis v R; Droudis v R* [2013] 249 CLR 92.

16 'Woman abused by trans-identified male contacted by police after "misgendering" non-binary patient while in hospital', *Reduxx*, 22 May 2023 (reduxx.info/woman-abused-by-trans-identified-male-contacted-by-police-after-misgendering-non-binary-patient-while-in-hospital).

of the *Public Order Act 1986* in England and Wales makes it an offence intentionally to cause a person "harassment, alarm or distress" by various means, including the use of abusive or insulting words. In April 2023, West Yorkshire police interviewed a woman in her seventies in her home after CCTV footage showed her taking a photograph. That photograph was not of a secret nuclear weapons depot, or an intelligence services file marked 'top secret'. It was a photograph of a small sticker that had been placed on a 'Trans Pride' poster. That sticker read "Keep Males Out Of Women-Only Spaces". She was lectured by the police regarding the "harassment and alarm" that this sticker could potentially cause the trans-identifying community. They recorded it as a "non-crime hate incident".[17] Police investigations of this kind can be experienced as harassment and can have a chilling effect on free speech, whether or not they result in charges being laid. In the great majority of cases, charges are not laid; if they are, prosecutors may decline to proceed with them.

As these examples indicate, issues concerning people who identify as transgender, non-binary or gender diverse are prominent in the current controversies about freedom of speech and allegedly hateful ideas. It seems unavoidable that claims to particular treatment on the basis of gender identity will clash with other human rights, and in particular the rights of women and girls to bodily privacy and safety. To some extent, these debates involve controversies about people's beliefs either concerning themselves specifically, or human biology generally. They may well challenge religious beliefs which accord with mainstream scientific understanding of human beings as a sexually dimorphic species. This is where transgender rights can come into conflict with religious freedom.[18] People of faith need the freedom to reject beliefs that are incompatible with their

---

17 Y Alma, 'UK: Senior woman interrogated by police after taking photograph of sticker critical of gender ideology', *Reduxx*, 26 August 2023 (reduxx.info/uk-senior-woman-interrogated-by-police-after-taking-photograph-of-sticker-critical-of-gender-ideology).

18 P Parkinson, 'Gender identity discrimination and religious freedom', *Journal of Law and Religion*, 26 January 2023, 38(1):10–37 (doi.org/10.1017/jlr.2022.45).

worldviews. This does not mean that ill-treatment or denigration of someone on the basis of their gender identity can ever be justified; but it may mean that a person of faith (or indeed science) is not in a position to accept someone's claims about themselves and to treat them accordingly. It is one thing to ask me to respect your beliefs about yourself; it is quite another to ask me to act toward you as if I share your beliefs.

Christian teaching as a form of terrorism

The Rev Dr Bernard Randall, the Chaplain at Trent College, an Anglican school in England, became somewhat alarmed by a professional development program for the teaching staff provided by an external organization in 2018. The leader of the program encouraged staff to chant "smash heteronormativity",[19] a slogan also used on the organization's website. The organization's program was subsequently rolled out to the students.[20]

While Dr Randall had no problem with some aspects of the educational program, he felt other aspects were impossible to reconcile with Christian teaching and therefore with the stated objectives for which the school was established. These objectives were to educate pupils "in accordance with the Protestant and Evangelical principles of the Church of England".[21] He decided to preach a chapel sermon in June 2019, the text of which he wrote out fully in advance. The topic of the sermon was 'competing ideologies'.[22] In it, he emphasized

---

19 This account is taken mainly from the 76-page judgement of the Employment Tribunal in *Randall v Trent College*, which rejected Randall's claim of discrimination, harassment, victimization and unfair dismissal. It is also taken from personal communications with Dr Randall.

20 'Educate & celebrate—smashing heteronormativity in the classroom', *Transgender Trend*, 23 June 2020 (transgendertrend.com/educate-celebrate-smashing-heteronormativity-classroom).

21 These objects do not now form part of the school's public statement about its vision and ethos.

22 The full text is available online at Christian Concern: 'A school sermon by Bernard Randall: Competing ideologies', 10 May 2021 (christianconcern.com/resource/a-school-sermon-by-bernard-randall-competing-ideologies).

that when ideologies compete, people should not descend into abuse, but should treat one another with respect for their different beliefs. He encouraged students to love the person, even when they profoundly dislike the ideas. Several times, he encouraged respect for those with whom we disagree.

He went on to discuss the potential conflict in values between the outside organization's program and religious values. He acknowledged that some of the program's statements were factual—for example, that there are same-sex-attracted people and people who experience gender dysphoria. There were other areas of overlap with Christian values—for example, that no-one should be discriminated against simply for who he or she is.

However, he also observed other areas where the two sets of ideas are in conflict—for example, on whether marriage should only be between a man and a woman, and whether sexual activity belongs only within such marriage. He told students that they did not have to accept the ideas and ideologies of LGBT activists, and that they were entitled to think that human beings are male and female, that sex cannot be changed, and that there are some real, biologically based differences between the sexes. On all such issues, he urged students to make up their own mind and not to feel as if they need to adhere to the beliefs and ideas being taught to them.

The sermon caused outrage. The school leadership received two formal complaints and a few other expressions of concern from staff or students. The concerns expressed were not only about the content. Some expressed the view that a chapel sermon was the wrong forum to deal with issues of this kind because there was no opportunity for questions or discussion. Others were concerned less about what Dr Randall had said than about the way it was heard or could be misinterpreted. Other criticisms were that the academic level of the sermon was too high for the children in the seventh and eighth grades to understand properly.

One might disagree with Dr Randall's sermon or have criticisms of the occasion for its delivery. But his message to students in an Anglican school was that it was alright to hold the beliefs and values that represent the official doctrine of the Church of England. As

Chaplain, he had a role in safeguarding the school's religious ethos and promoting Christian values.

However, the woman who was the school's designated 'safeguarding lead' felt so strongly about Dr Randall's views that she referred his sermon, with an accompanying note, to Prevent, a government-led, multi-agency program that aims to stop individuals becoming radicalized and engaging in terrorism. Unsurprisingly, the anti-terrorism group did not take the matter further.

Neither she nor any of the other school leaders had, it seems, been concerned about the training organization that had encouraged teachers to "smash heteronormativity". Of course, the leader's incitement of staff to violence was only metaphorical, and the chanting might not have been intended as a radicalizing technique. However, it was at least a little more violent than a bespectacled Anglican clergyman telling students that it was alright for them to hold to Anglican doctrine and to reject other beliefs if they were unpersuaded by them.

In the aftermath of this sermon, Dr Randall was dismissed for gross misconduct, although he was subsequently reinstated on appeal to the governors, subject to compliance with various management instructions. He was made redundant a year or so later. His legal actions against the school were all rejected by the Employment Tribunal. It supported the referral to Prevent as reasonable in the circumstances. At time of writing, Dr Randall has successfully appealed this decision and the case has been sent back for rehearing.

As another illustration of how redefining child protection can be weaponized against someone on the grounds of their religious beliefs (see chapter 2), Dr Randall's diocesan safeguarding team reached the view—without evidence, and without following official guidance—that he was a safeguarding risk to children. This was not the view taken by secular authorities responsible for safeguarding, nor by a senior legal officer of the Church asked to review the case. There was no evidence that Dr Randall had behaved inappropriately with children, either in his pastoral ministry at Trent College or previously. It appeared that doctrinal differences had improperly influenced the safeguarding team's decisions. The bishop refused to renew Dr Randall's licence to exercise ministry, and the controversy eventually embroiled the Archbishop of Canterbury.[23]

It is possible that the identification of Christian teaching with extremism and radicalization will become more common in future, at least in English-speaking countries. In 2021, the *Terrorism (Community Protection) Act 2003* was amended in Victoria to give the government extensive powers to intervene in relation to people deemed to be "radicalising towards violent extremism".[24] The approach taken is a therapeutic one, to help the person by addressing what are seen to be the underlying causes of radicalization. It relies, in the first instance, on the person giving his or her informed consent. However, if that consent is not forthcoming or is withdrawn, it is possible for police to seek a "support and engagement" order from a court. Breach of such an order has consequences. It is an offence to contravene an order without a reasonable excuse.[25]

What is the definition of "radicalising towards violent extremism"? Surprisingly, no indication of any tendency towards committing a terrorist act is required.[26] It may be enough that the person has disseminated or endorsed statements expressing hatred, serious contempt, revulsion or severe ridicule of the public or a section of the public, or has engaged in racial or religious vilification for the purposes of advancing a political, religious or ideological cause.[27]

Could such a law be weaponized by someone intent on arguing that disseminating or endorsing religious beliefs—perhaps about a contested matter such as same-sex relationships or gender identity—indicates that the person complained about is on a pathway towards violent extremism? At present, there are sufficient procedural safeguards in the legislation to make it unlikely that this law could be successfully weaponized in this way. But who would

---

23 'Archbishop "whitewashed" complaint in "egregious" blacklisting case', *Christian Concern*, 13 August 2024 (christianconcern.com/news/welby-whitewashed-safeguarding-failure-that-led-to-chaplains-blacklisting).

24 *Terrorism (Community Protection) Act 2003 (Vic)*, s 4A.

25 *Terrorism (Community Protection) Act 2003 (Vic)*, s 22CU.

26 *Terrorism (Community Protection) Act 2003 (Vic)*, s 22AG(2).

27 *Terrorism (Community Protection) Act 2003 (Vic)*, s 22AG(3) and (4).

have thought that a legal tribunal in England, with knowledge of all the facts and circumstances, could have seen the referral of Bernard Randall to anti-terrorism authorities as reasonable? The way in which the term "hate speech" has been given such a broad interpretation by activists who have their own political or ideological causes makes it likely that such "hate speech" complaints will be made to the police and other relevant authorities, using whatever legislation is available for the purpose.

The Australian Human Rights Commission also appears to endorse the position that people who hold certain kinds of viewpoint on LGBTQ+ issues are extremists. The Commission, which is entrusted with promoting and guarding all human rights, launched an inquiry into threats to the rights of trans-identifying people and those who identify as 'gender diverse'.[28] Among its terms of reference were to examine "anti-trans mobilisation, dis- and misinformation, and extremism and radicalisation". The Commission did not show any intention of considering how the rights of trans- or gender-diverse-identifying people might be balanced with the rights of others in cases of conflict—in particular, the rights of women and girls to single-sex facilities and competitions.

This would appear to be reflective of an international trend over the last few years. In March 2024, the British government released a new definition of extremism for the purposes of its governmental work.[29] Extremism is now defined, inter alia, as the promotion or advancement of an ideology based on violence, hatred or intolerance, that aims to negate or destroy the fundamental rights and freedoms of others. The inclusion of 'intolerance' towards the rights of others gives the definition a very broad scope that could, at a future time, be weaponized against mainstream religious beliefs.

In New Zealand, an organization called the Christchurch Call was established as a collaboration between government and

---

28 Australian Human Rights Commission, 'Current and emerging threats to TGD human rights', AHRC website (humanrights.gov.au/have-your-say/current-and-emerging-threats-tgd-human-rights).

29 'Guidance: New definition of extremism (2024)', *Gov.UK* (www.gov.uk/government/publications/new-definition-of-extremism-2024).

non-government organizations, including technology companies, to address issues of terrorism in the wake of the Christchurch massacre. Fifty-one Muslims were shot dead at two mosques in March 2019 by an Australian man who was motivated by anger at terrorist attacks and other crimes by non-white people in Australia and elsewhere. The work of the Christchurch Call has been criticized on the basis of 'mission creep', because its agenda includes 'gender-based hate', including in relation to issues of gender identity, and dissent from ideologies that promote diversity and inclusion.[30]

The degree of 'definition inflation' in labelling people potential terrorists represents a significant threat to the religious freedom of those who hold conservative positions on LGBTQ+ issues. In many countries, the prevention of terrorism justifies laws that would otherwise be seen as unjustifiable forms of interference with basic civil liberties, and which modify the normal protections available to people suspected of, or charged with, criminal offences. There is the world of difference between conspiring with others to plant an explosive device that could kill hundreds of people, and opposing societal changes about human sexuality or diversity of gender identity.

Conversion therapy laws

Another kind of law that could be weaponized against people of faith is one that purports to prohibit 'conversion therapy'. Such laws have been an insistent demand of LGBTQ+ advocacy groups. The ostensible justification for these laws is to criminalize forms of therapy provided by medical and mental-health professionals that seek to change a person's sexual orientation—whether or not the person asks for, or consents to, the treatment.

The conversion therapy law in Queensland provides some examples of the kinds of therapy that are banned. These include inducing

---

30 See 'Stop Christchurch Call from Silencing Kiwis', *Free Speech Union* (www.fsu.nz/ stop_christchurch_call_from_silencing_kiwis).

nausea, vomiting or paralysis while showing the person same-sex images, or using shame or coercion to give the person an aversion to same-sex attractions.[31] Such practices disappeared from medical and mental-health practices many decades ago, and are now widely regarded both as unethical and ineffective. Such practices, if ever now utilised, would almost certainly lead to disciplinary action by the regulatory authorities, as well as exposing the practitioner to negligence claims.

If conversion therapy laws had been confined to such outdated and discredited practices, they might have been considered entirely unnecessary, but otherwise uncontroversial. However, typically they extend to gender identity as well. This is much more controversial, for three reasons.

First, the evidence is very weak that gender identity is innate and unchangeable. Even among leading practitioners in gender clinics, it is accepted that gender identity may not be fixed. In a seminal article on so-called 'gender-affirming care', clinicians from four gender-identity clinics in the USA explained their belief that "gender may be fluid, and is not binary, both at a particular time and if and when it changes within an individual across time".[32]

Secondly, there is no evidence that the therapeutic interventions practised in the past to help children, young people and adults to deal with gender incongruence have been harmful. There is consequently no justification for criminalizing a particular kind of therapy.

Third, there is mounting evidence that gender incongruence is associated with being on the autism spectrum and with adverse childhood experiences such as family dysfunction, family breakdown and child abuse.[33] This would point to therapeutic approaches being most appropriate.

31 *Public Health Act 2005*, s 213F.
32 MA Hidalgo et al., 'The gender affirmative model: what we know and what we aim to learn', *Human Development*, 29 October 2013, 56(5):285 (karger.com/hde/article/56/5/285/157895/The-Gender-Affirmative-Model-What-We-Know-and-What).
33 See, for example, K Kozlowska et al., 'Australian children and adolescents with gender dysphoria: Clinical presentations and challenges experienced by a multi-disciplinary team and gender service', 22 April 2021, *Human Systems*, 1(1):70–95 (doi.org/10.1177/26344041211010777).

Conversion therapy laws may also apply to practices that are unrelated to therapeutic methods used in the long distant past by mental health professionals. In several jurisdictions, these laws are applicable to the general community, not just health professionals. In Victoria, a 2021 law makes it a criminal offence, if certain conditions are satisfied,[34] for someone to pray with another person to "change or suppress" their sexual orientation or gender identity. The penalty is up to ten years in jail. The legislation also gives coercive powers to the state's Equal Opportunity and Human Rights Commission to investigate people suspected of engaging in such practices and to enforce undertakings not to do so in future.

Consider what this means. A churchgoer in Victoria could approach their pastor and say, "I am struggling with my gender identity. Would you pray with me that God would take away this sense of confusion?" Victorian law makes it illegal for the pastor to do so. If he is to obey the law, he must refuse to pray with a member of his congregation who asks for prayer. That is a red line when it comes to religious freedom.

Victoria, like many other jurisdictions, also makes it an offence to engage in any practice that would "suppress" a sexual orientation or gender identity. Thus prayer, or any form of therapy, directed to assist a person to suppress an unwanted same-sex attraction in order to live life as a heterosexual, will contravene the law, even if that assistance is earnestly sought by the person concerned. The law could even be applied to counselling that advocates heterosexual celibacy for someone who is unmarried, since the definition of sexual orientation includes either a heterosexual or same-sex attraction.[35]

---

34 *Change or Suppression (Conversion) Practices Prohibition Act 2021*, s 10, 11. A criminal offence is committed if three conditions are satisfied. First, the defendant intentionally engages in the prohibited change or suppression practice. Second, injury is caused to the person concerned. Third, the defendant is negligent as to whether the practice will cause injury to the person concerned. Injury is defined (in the *Crimes Act 1958* (Vic) s 15) as physical injury or harm to mental health, whether temporary or permanent.

35 The definition is the same as in section 4 of the *Equal Opportunity Act 2010*. It "means a person's emotional, affectional and sexual attraction to, or intimate or sexual relations with, persons of a different gender or the same gender or more than one gender".

The Victorian Equal Opportunity and Human Rights Commission, which is empowered to implement the law, gives several specific examples on its website of religious practices that it says contravene the law. These include: "a religious leader meeting one-on-one and telling a member of their congregation that they are broken and pressuring them to suppress and ignore their feelings of same-sex attraction by practising celibacy"; "a religious leader telling a member of their congregation—with the intent to induce that person to change or suppress their sexuality—that they will be excommunicated if they continue their same-sex relationship and prohibited from returning as long as that relationship continues" and "using a youth group session to provide 'support' through group prayer to a young person to help them fight a desire to act on their feelings of same-sex attraction".[36] These examples provide an extended application of the idea of a 'conversion practice'.

Even if a prosecutor were to consider such an extended meaning of a conversion practice to fall within the law, it would be necessary for him or her to be able to prove two other factors beyond reasonable doubt: that injury is caused to the person concerned; and that the person being prosecuted was negligent as to whether the practice will cause injury to that person.

The Commission's guidance on the interpretation of the law also illustrates how laws of this kind can be weaponized by activists in government agencies. By purporting to say how the law should be interpreted and applied, and taking the broadest possible view of the legislative language, activists can seek to give members of the community the impression that the law is much more threatening than it really is. So, for example, the Commission even offers detailed guidance to people of faith on how they are allowed to pray for someone who is same-sex attracted. They are not allowed to ask for healing for that person, even at their request. Nor can they pray for that person to not act on their attractions or to be helped

---

36 Equal Opportunity and Human Rights Commission, 'Have you experienced a change or suppression practice?' Victorian Equal Opportunity and Human Rights Commission website (humanrights.vic.gov.au/change-or-suppression-practices/have-you-experienced-a-change-or-suppression-practice).

to maintain long-term celibacy. The guidance purports to cover not only prayers with a same-sex attracted person, but even prayers that are prayed without them being present. In their benevolence, the Commission assures us that there is "a broad range of prayers that would be acceptable and supportive". In Victoria, before praying for someone who is struggling with same-sex attraction, make sure you submit your draft prayer to the government for approval.

Whatever disagreements Christians may have about how to deal with the variety of pastoral and theological issues concerning same-sex relationships, we can all perhaps agree that it is absurd for government officials, who may not even believe in a divine being or in the power of prayer, to draw up a detailed list of what we can and cannot pray for on our own in the privacy of our own homes. Such a law far exceeds the legitimate role of government. As Catholic Archbishop Comensoli of Melbourne put it: "Who I pray to, how I pray, what I pray for, and most particularly, who I pray with is not of concern to any government".[37]

The Commission's guidance also goes far beyond what the law actually says. There is no chance whatsoever of a successful prosecution in Victoria based upon what someone prays for when they are alone and in private. It is a basic principle of statutory interpretation that criminal laws need to be read restrictively—that is, in a narrow and limited manner—and that Parliament does not intend to deprive people of their basic human rights. Nor is it likely that the Commission would pursue other means of enforcement available to it in such circumstances. It would risk a huge backlash against the agency.

However, people of faith may be misled by such activist interpretations to believe that governments have a right to determine what you pray for and with whom you pray. Guidance of this kind is all part of the activist playbook.

37 F Tomazin, 'Gay conversion legislation puts Andrews on a collision course with churches', *The Age*, 5 December 2020 (theage.com.au/politics/victoria/gay-conversion-legislation-puts-andrews-on-a-collision-course-with-churches-20201204-p56ks6.html).

4

RELIGIOUS FREEDOM AS
A HUMAN RIGHT

*Why do many human-rights laws provide limited
protection for religious freedom?*

People of faith have long been in the vanguard of movements to
promote human rights, not only to protect freedom to proclaim the
gospel (1 Tim 2:1–4), but also to promote the equal treatment of
people. The great American civil rights leader Martin Luther King
was a clergyman. Other Christians have also been prominent in
the civil rights movement. Christianity brought to the world a radical understanding of equality because of the position we all stand
in—all having sinned and fallen short of the glory of God (Rom 3:23),
but all being given equal access to the throne of grace in Christ. The
apostle Paul wrote: "There is neither Jew nor Greek, neither slave nor
free, nor is there male and female, for you are all one in Christ Jesus"
(Gal 3:28). This radical proposition about equality in the kingdom of
God has, for many, led to a Christian commitment to equality on
earth as in heaven.

Concern for the dignity of all human beings, whatever their status or situation in life, provides a reason for Christians to support
movements for the promotion of human rights, especially in the
many countries of the world where governments routinely and egre-
giously violate the rights of citizens. That support for human rights

must nonetheless be balanced by a recognition that in the New Testament, we are called to the fulfilment of responsibilities and care for others, rather than claiming 'rights'. Jesus laid down his rights for the sake of others (Phil 2:5–8). Christians cannot support the narcissistic focus of some advocates on rights for themselves at the expense of other people's rights and needs.

Religious freedom as a fundamental human right

Over 170 countries are signatories to the International Covenant on Civil and Political Rights (ICCPR). The ICCPR obliges governments to protect a number of rights and freedoms that are essential to a free and just society. Article 18 of the ICCPR protects freedom of thought, conscience and religion. This is a right that, the ICCPR says, governments cannot depart from even in a time of national emergency.[1]

The right to freedom of religion cannot be understood in isolation from four other freedoms: freedom of conscience, of expression, of assembly, and of association.[2] If we have freedom to worship but not freedom to teach our doctrines or witness to our faith, then our freedom is little more than has been permitted in communist countries where religious freedom has been greatly restricted. The right of believers to meet in corporate worship requires freedom of assembly. If we do not have freedom of association, then governments can restrict the freedoms of any religious organization to govern itself in accordance with its beliefs—for example, in determining who should be allowed into, or excluded from, membership, or in determining staffing policies in a faith-based organization. If we have freedom to worship but employers are under no obligation to make any accommodations for conscience, then we are likely to face restrictions upon the jobs we can take—for example, in the health professions.

Freedom of conscience is, of course, closely related to freedom of religion. The UN Human Rights Committee has sought to draw to the attention of governments "the fact that the freedom of thought

---

1   Article 4(2).
2   ICCPR, articles 18, 19, 21 and 22 respectively.

and the freedom of conscience are protected equally with the freedom of religion and belief".[3] Respecting freedom of religion means
accommodating faith-based observances and conscientious objections, as far as possible, but within reasonable limits.

The work of freedom of religion, then, requires us also to stand up
for other freedoms, including when enjoyed by those whose worldview or lifestyle we do not necessarily share. That is particularly
important in a multicultural society, where there must be tolerance
for different values and beliefs. The implicit multicultural compact is
that we should live and let live, and that we should allow one another
the freedom to be different from whatever represents the prevailing
majority viewpoint on such issues as sexuality and family life.

Like many freedoms, freedom of religion has certain components
that are not absolute; it is qualified to some extent. The right to
believe what one chooses is as absolute as the right to freedom of
thought. But the manifestation of religious belief is subject to limitations. These are set out in Article 18.3 of the ICCPR. The right to
manifest a religion or belief can be limited by law where necessary
to protect public safety, order, health, or morals, or the fundamental
rights and freedoms of others.

The UN Commission on Human Rights has given its formal
acknowledgment to a set of principles developed in the mid-1980s
by a group of distinguished international law experts for interpreting these terms. These are known as the Siracusa Principles.[4] They
emphasize that the scope of a limitation referred to in the ICCPR
should not be interpreted so as to jeopardize the essence of the
right concerned. That is, governments cannot deprive people of the
right to religious freedom in order to advance some other purpose.
Rights can be restricted, but not taken away. To similar effect, the

3   UN Human Rights Committee, 'General Comment No. 22: Article 18 (Freedom of
    Thought, Conscience or Religion)', *Refworld*, 30 July 1993, paragraph 1 (refworld.
    org/legal/general/hrc/1993/en/13375).

4   American Association for the International Commission of Jurists, 'Siracusa
    Principles on the Limitation and Derogation Provisions in the International Covenant
    on Civil and Political Rights', 1985 (icj.org/resource/siracusa-principles-on-the-
    limitation-and-derogation-provisions-in-the-international-covenant-on-civil-
    and-political-rights).

UN Human Rights Committee, which adjudicates on alleged human-rights violations by countries that are signatories to the ICCPR, has made it clear that limitations must not be applied in a manner that would vitiate the right to freedom of religion.[5]

Another important document on religious freedom is the Declaration on the Elimination of All Forms of Intolerance and of Discrimination Based on Religion or Belief. Adopted unanimously by the UN General Assembly in 1981, the Declaration sets out what is involved in protecting religious belief and practice. Article 6 provides that, subject to relevant limitations, the right to freedom of thought, conscience, religion or belief shall include a range of specific rights. These include the right to establish and maintain appropriate charitable or humanitarian institutions, to disseminate religious publications, and to train and appoint appropriate leaders called for by the requirements and standards of any religion or belief. Some of the freedoms listed are not under threat in Western nations. Others, however, are, to a greater or lesser extent, under threat, or subject to significant constraints. This may seem surprising, given the prominence of the idea of human rights in modern Western societies.

Why is this so? To understand this, it is necessary to delve further into the discourse on human rights and the different ways in which they can be protected in law.

Entrenched safeguards for human rights

In some countries, certain human rights are protected by constitutional guarantees. These are known as 'entrenched' protections. They allow the courts to declare invalid any law, or section within a law, that is found to violate a human right protected in the Constitution. The best-known example is the US Constitution. The First Amendment provides:

> Congress shall make no law respecting an establishment of religion, or prohibiting the free exercise thereof; or abridging the freedom of speech, or of the press; or the right of the

5   'General Comment No. 22: Article 18', paragraph 8.

people peaceably to assemble, and to petition the Government for a redress of grievances.[6]

Here, just one clause guarantees five freedoms in all: freedom of religion, freedom of the press, freedom of speech, freedom of assembly and freedom of petition. Although the US Constitution was written only to govern the federation of individual States that came to comprise the United States of America, the guarantees of freedoms contained in the First Amendment have been applied to state laws and local government as well. They do not apply to private organizations or businesses.

The First Amendment provides very strong constitutional guarantees. Over many years, the Supreme Court of the United States (SCOTUS) has refined its principles for how such rights and freedoms are to be interpreted and applied when they come into conflict with legitimate public interests, such as public health. If a law, while stated to be of general application, is really targeted at a religious practice, it will attract strict scrutiny from the Court.[7] However, if a law is of general application and does not single out religion, it is unlikely that religious objectors will successfully be able to challenge it. Provided the law has a legitimate purpose, and is a rational means of achieving that purpose, it will remain valid even if it has an adverse effect on freedom of religion.[8]

Policies of a government entity, including a public university, are subject to scrutiny on a similar basis. If a policy is of general application, it will not be seen as infringing freedom of religion. An example is SCOTUS's decision in *Christian Legal Society v Martinez*, decided in 2010.[9] The case concerned a Christian student group that wished to be officially recognized at Hastings Law School, which comes under the University of California. Being a public university, First Amendment protections apply.

6   'The Bill of Rights: A Transcription', *National Archives* (archives.gov/founding-docs/bill-of-rights-transcript).
7   *Church of the Lukumi Babalu Aye, Inc. v City of Hialeah* [1993] 508 US 520, 542–43, 546.
8   *Employment Division v Smith* [1990] 494 US 872.
9   [2010] 561 US 661.

The Christian Legal Society, as is common for many Christian student groups, required members and officers to sign their agreement to the group's statement of beliefs, which also included a commitment to live by certain principles, including that sexual activity should not occur outside of marriage between a man and a woman. This conflicted with the law school's "all-comers" policy, under which the school would only recognize (and therefore give financial support to) student groups that "'allow any student to participate, become a member, or seek leadership positions in the organization", regardless of their status or beliefs.

By a 5–4 majority, SCOTUS held that the policy did not infringe the religious freedom rights of the Christian student group because it was of general application. The argument, so far as it concerned funding, was that no student should be forced to fund a group that would reject her as a member. There was a sharp difference between the majority and the minority concerning the relevant facts of the case, with the minority arguing there was a quite selective application of policy by the Law School in a way that targeted the religious group. However, the majority found that the all-comers policy applied to all organizations, whether religious or political.

By way of contrast, SCOTUS upheld the right of Catholic Social Services to continue to provide foster care services to the City of Philadelphia, even though it maintained the position that unmarried couples (regardless of their sexual orientation) or same-sex married couples seeking to foster should be referred to another agency.[10] This, according to the City, contravened its non-discrimination policies. SCOTUS unanimously held that the City's policy infringed on the religious liberty rights of Catholic Social Services because it was not of general application. The policy allowed for agencies to exclude prospective foster or adoptive parents based upon their sexual orientation if the Commissioner or the Commissioner's delegate granted an exception in his or her sole discretion. That took the policy outside one of general application.

A further principle is that a law that, on its face, is neutral must

---

10 *Fulton v City of Philadelphia* [2021] 141 S. Ct. 1868.

not be enforced against people of faith in a way that violates the principle of state neutrality on religious matters.[11] As Chief Justice Roberts explained in one case, "Government fails to act neutrally when it proceeds in a manner intolerant of religious beliefs or restricts practices because of their religious nature".[12]

The First Amendment protections for religious freedom are limited in scope; but they do provide a measure of protection for many of the rights set out in the Declaration on the Elimination of All Forms of Intolerance and of Discrimination Based on Religion or Belief. That cannot be said for the human-rights guarantees, such as they are, in many other countries.

Statutory charters of human rights

The United States offers stronger protections for human rights than many other countries. In Europe, human rights are guaranteed by the European Convention for the Protection of Human Rights and Fundamental Freedoms, to which the 46 nations of the Council of Europe are signatories. Responsibility for implementing the Convention rests with the Parliaments and courts of member states. So, for example, in Britain, the Convention is given statutory force through the *Human Rights Act 1998*, and it is this law that is applied in British courts.[13]

Where someone believes that their government is not compliant with the Convention, a case can be brought to the European Court of Human Rights in Strasbourg after domestic remedies have been exhausted. The European Court has built up a large body of case law on the interpretation and application of the Convention, including in relation to religious freedom. However, the European Court allows member nations a substantial 'margin of appreciation' concerning how to implement the Convention. This means that the way one country balances different rights may be quite different from a neighbouring country, with each country being allowed some

11 *Masterpiece Cakeshop, Ltd. v Colorado Civil Rights Commission* [2018] 138 S. Ct. 1719.

12 *Fulton v City of Philadelphia* [2021] 141 S. Ct. 1877.

13 The UK has remained a member of the Council of Europe even after leaving the EU.

freedom to make decisions that best suit its circumstances. This 'margin of appreciation' doctrine leaves at least some room for each country to chart its own pathway. But the European Court provides a unifying set of principles and a body of case law that can guide the interpretation of domestic laws.

In Australia, Victoria, Queensland and the Australian Capital Territory (the small part of the country where the capital, Canberra, is situated) have statutory charters of human rights;[14] but these are more limited in their effectiveness than in Europe. This is because in practice they are largely advisory. The situation is similar in New Zealand.[15] New bills are scrutinized for compliance with the human-rights standards of the charter, to draw attention to obvious inconsistency. Also, a court may declare that a particular provision in a statute is incompatible with a right defined in the jurisdiction's Human Rights Act, but this will not strike down the provision. The parliament is alerted to the issue, and ordinary parliamentary processes determine whether to change the law in light of the court's ruling.[16] In this way, the supremacy of Parliament is maintained. The mere fact that a court declares the offending law to be incompatible with a charter of human rights is therefore not enough to change the offending law.

The three charters enacted in Australia are, however, not well-aligned with the ICCPR. Among other things, they authorize the restriction of religious freedom and other rights for reasons that are much broader than those "necessary to protect public safety, order, health, or morals or the fundamental rights and freedoms of others" (article 18.3, ICCPR). The charters also do not define rights in the same way as the ICCPR, and freedom of religion is one of the rights worst affected. Charters are therefore not consistent with Australia's international human-rights obligations, especially insofar as the protection of religious freedom is concerned. For example, in contrast with the word 'necessary' in article 18, section 7(2) of the

---

14   *Human Rights Act 2004* (ACT), *Charter of Human Rights and Responsibilities Act 2006* (Vic), *Human Rights Act 2019* (Qld).

15   *New Zealand Bill of Rights Act 1990.*

16   This is why these charters are described as a "dialogue" model.

Victorian *Charter of Rights and Responsibilities Act 2006* provides:

> A human right may be subject under law only to such reasonable limits as can be demonstrably justified in a free and democratic society based on human dignity, equality and freedom, and taking into account all relevant factors including—
>
> - the nature of the right; and
> - the importance of the purpose of the limitation; and
> - the nature and extent of the limitation; and
> - the relationship between the limitation and its purpose; and
> - any less restrictive means reasonably available to achieve the purpose that the limitation seeks to achieve.

So, any of the enumerated rights can be restricted without consequence, as long as the court considers that the limits placed upon the exercise of that right are reasonable. In any event, a declaration that any legislation is incompatible with a charter right does not bind the government of the day to propose corrective legislation.

When some rights are more equal than others

Rarely, in practice, is there an issue about whether the restriction of a human right is reasonable in isolation from competing considerations. The competing factor may be an important public interest, such as community health during an outbreak of infectious disease; or, as is so often the case, the human rights of others. As has been noted above, the right to have a religious belief is absolute; but the right to *manifest* one's religious belief in the community is subject to limitations.

A fundamental mantra of human-rights advocates and human-rights commissions charged with upholding rights is that human rights are "universal, indivisible and interdependent and interrelated".[17] All human rights relevant to an issue ought to be considered together; and one right should not be emphasized to such an extent that it

---

17   United Nations Human Rights, Office of the High Commissioner, 'Vienna Declaration and Programme of Action', *United Nations*, 12 July 1993 (www.ohchr.org/en/instruments-mechanisms/instruments/vienna-declaration-and-programme-action).

unjustifiably trespasses on another right. When considering whether a human right can be limited, the approach taken is that restrictions on the enjoyment of a right must be "proportionate" to the legitimate aim pursued, applying objective considerations.

However, in a conflict between rights, policy choices embedded in legislation often drive the outcome, favouring some rights over others. The effect of a particular law may be to diminish one right in order to elevate another right, or even for one right to trump another right. This choice between rights is almost inevitable.

A contemporary illustration is the clash between the rights asserted in some situations by men who identify as 'transgender women', and the rights of girls and women when it comes to single-sex facilities. In the United States, several states have passed so-called 'bathroom laws', requiring students to use the bathrooms and changing rooms of their biological sex.

The conflict of rights is particularly acute when male students who identify as female want to use female changing rooms, affecting the rights of female students, including the right to personal privacy. Should the rights of women and girls to single-sex spaces take precedence over males who assert a female gender identity (or vice versa)? No matter how committed a person is to LGBTQ+ rights or non-discrimination generally, the issues can look very different for the parent of a teenage daughter required to share a changing room or sleeping accommodation at a camp with a male who now identifies as female.

The Biden Administration drew up federal regulations requiring schools that receive federal funding not to "discriminate" against transgender students. In stark contrast, the second Trump Administration issued a strong Executive Order on the issue, stating that the US government will recognize "two sexes, male and female", and that "these sexes are not changeable and are grounded in fundamental and incontrovertible reality".[18] The Trump Administration's

---

18 'Defending women from gender ideology extremism and restoring biological truth to the Federal Government', *The White House*, 20 January 2025 (whitehouse.gov/presidential-actions/2025/01/defending-women-from-gender-ideology-extremism-and-restoring-biological-truth-to-the-federal-government).

Executive Orders have done much to wind back transgender rights, but, at the time of writing, are subject to challenge in the courts.

No amount of talk about 'balancing' rights can resolve the need to make a stark choice between conflicting rights and interests when they represent irreconcilable alternatives. The path of wisdom in this area is arguably to make no rule at all—let the school management work out each situation as it arises in consultation with all the students affected and their parents, perhaps by making available a gender-neutral toilet or changing area for the trans-identifying person.

It is, of course, entirely legitimate for parliaments to choose which rule to enact, if any. But when this analysis is cloaked in the language of 'human rights', it is often presented as a policy change required by something called 'international human-rights law'. Much of the time, reference by human-rights interest groups to 'international human-rights law' merely involves the unprincipled cherry-picking of decisions from various courts around the world. Another strategy is to identify a human right as 'emerging', because it is recognized in the laws of countries that conform to the organization's preferred policy. The sometimes esoteric and abstract language of human-rights analysis disguises political advocacy. Increasingly, that advocacy comes from an anti-Christian, or anti-faith, worldview.

An example of how the language of 'human rights' cloaks personal preferences and viewpoints is the Australian Law Reform Commission's 2024 report on removing exemptions for religious educational institutions from anti-discrimination laws.[19] This inquiry was established to fulfil an election commitment to amend the law so that, in faith-based schools, the rights of students or staff who identify as gay, lesbian, bisexual or transgender should prevail over the rights of the school to maintain its religious identity, ethos and values where these conflict. The policy also provided that faith-based schools could give preference to persons of the same religion as the school when selecting staff.

19 Australian Law Reform Commission, 'Final Report: Maximising the realisation of human rights: Religious educational institutions and anti-discrimination laws', *Australian Government*, 21 March 2024 (alrc.gov.au/publication/adl-report-142).

The Terms of Reference given to the Australian Law Reform Commission (ALRC) required it to come up with legislative recommendations to enact this policy that would be consistent, as far as possible, with Australia's international human-rights commitments. The report strived to present an impression of how this could be done in a way that would make almost everyone happy. It was entitled "Maximising the Realisation of Human Rights". On its front page, ten rights and freedoms are listed, and at the bottom, in italics is the following: "Human rights are indivisible and interdependent in nature. Woven together, human rights reinforce each other and promote the enjoyment of all rights and human flourishing."

This makes it sound as if the ALRC's task was just to make sure that all the relevant human rights should be applied in way that maximizes rights for everyone. Furthermore, the Commission made clear that it was treating all human rights as equal.[20]

However, not unlike the situation that George Orwell described in *Animal Farm*, some rights turn out to be more equal than others. As the Commission went on to explain:

> The ALRC has concluded that the recommended reforms may limit, for some people, the freedom to manifest religion or belief in community with others, and the associated parental liberty to ensure the religious and moral education of their children in conformity with their own convictions.[21]

Not too much maximizing of human rights there.[22] The Commission went on to recommend restrictions on the right of faith-based schools to give preference in the appointment of staff to people who

20 ALRC, 'Final Report', p 36 (principle 2).
21 ALRC, 'Final Report', p 98.
22 See the UN Human Rights Committee's General Comment No. 22: "The freedom from coercion to have or to adopt a religion or belief and the liberty of parents and guardians to ensure religious and moral education cannot be restricted". Office of the High Commissioner for Human Rights, 'General Comment No. 22: The right to freedom of thought, conscience and religion', Equal Rights Trust website, 1993, paragraph 8 (equalrightstrust.org/ertdocumentbank/general%20comment%2022. pdf). The Commission's position is arguably inconsistent with this insofar as its recommendations affect parents' choice of schools.

share the faith commitment of the school, thereby diminishing the freedoms they have long enjoyed. Christian schools, said the Commission, can only prefer to appoint Christian staff if such preference "is reasonably necessary to build or maintain a community of faith" and is proportionate to that aim, taking account of any disadvantage or harm that may be caused to any people not preferred.[23] This could make the staffing policies of Christian schools subject to constant litigation about whether they could justify a preference for employing committed Christians as teachers.

The effect of the Law Reform Commission's recommendations is that faith-based schools should be restricted in their staffing policies in order to allow non-religious teachers to have a wider choice of teaching jobs. Non-religious organizations established for a particular purpose or cause, such as an environmental organization, are under no such constraints. Political parties, likewise, are not subject to court scrutiny over whether they prefer staff who share the purposes and values of the party. Why is religion being singled out?

The ALRC did not claim that its recommendations were the only ones that could be consistent with international human rights; they only claimed it was one way of giving effect to Australia's human-rights commitments.[24] Its recommendations involved choices and value judgements. For example, it said:

> The evidence available to the ALRC suggests that any detriment to religious educational institutions under [the recommended reforms] would be minor, and would be less significant than detriments experienced by students and staff in religious educational institutions under existing legislative exceptions.[25]

That conclusion involved rejecting views expressed in submissions by a great many people of faith, including organizations representing faith-based schools, which were concerned about the impact of changes to the law on their ability to retain their religious identity and ethos.

23 ALRC, 'Final Report', p 15 (recommendation 7).
24 ALRC, 'Final Report', p 117.
25 ALRC, 'Final Report', p 100.

This example illustrates how hidden within claims about treating all rights as equal, or 'maximizing' rights, are value judgements about which rights should be given preference over other rights. A particular blind spot of human-rights organizations is their focus on the rights of individuals as contrasted with the rights of communities. Faith is expressed communally, and religious freedom really cannot be understood without acknowledging that it is exercised within a community of other believers. However, human-rights discourse is highly individualistic, especially as it is translated into anti-discrimination laws. It is the individual, not the community of faith, who is protected under these laws.

Soon after the report was published, the distinguished judge who led the inquiry disavowed some of its recommendations, saying that if he had not been constrained by the Terms of Reference, he would have recommended that faith-based schools be given a "positive right" to hire staff based on their ethos.[26] He argued that faith-based schools should be able to choose staff, or give a preference, on the basis of the person's adherence to or belief in the genuinely held religious beliefs or tenets of the school. That right should override state or federal laws to the contrary—even as it should be subject to constraints that the school must not discriminate against a student or staff unreasonably on the basis of a characteristic that would otherwise receive protection under anti-discrimination laws. The judge himself is a man of faith. Given the freedom to choose what application of 'international human rights' he would have regarded as most suitable in the circumstances, he would have made recommendations profoundly different from those made in the ALRC report.

Human-rights charters and the interpretive community

Human-rights advocates seek to give the impression that there is an ordered and objective process of reasoning from human-rights

26 The relevant passages of Justice Rothman's speech have been set out, with the judge's permission, in a paper by Mark Fowler given to the Australian Association of Christian Schools: 'The international context for religious freedom', 30 May 2024 (aacs.net.au/pdf/Fowler%20-%20CSA%20Speech%20300524.pdf).

principles to the way laws should be written. But in truth, much depends on who is interpreting and applying those principles, and which rights they consider to be more equal than others. In countries such as the United States, with a body of Supreme Court decisions made over many decades, and a sophisticated process for balancing different rights, the interpretive community combines those now holding judicial office with those who went before. The system requires current judges to take account of past wisdom and precedent. Change—sometimes radical change—occurs, but the past acts as a constraint upon the judges of the present; it keeps them from simply deciding matters according to their personal values.

However, where there is not such a strong system of binding precedent—including in Europe, where countries are given a wide 'margin of appreciation' to decide what weight to give to one human right when it conflicts with another—the values of those interpreting "human-rights law" are particularly important.

In recent years, there has been a distinct shift in the position of official human-rights organizations and advocacy groups to elevate non-discrimination as the highest value. This position has been particularly strongly held in terms of employment, with some arguing that all jobs should be open to all people who have the requisite formal qualifications unless a particular characteristic is an inherent requirement of the position (e.g. being of Indian female appearance to play the role of an Indian woman in a film). This means that the rights of religious organizations to maintain their identity as faith-based communities—to be religious, in fact—have gradually been diminished in favour of others' rights to work in religious organizations.

This produces an inversion of the guarantees that the original drafters of the ICCPR had established. Article 18.3 says that freedom of religion can be limited by law where necessary to protect the fundamental rights and freedoms of others. The word 'necessary' sets a high bar: only such limitations that can manifestly be justified as *necessary* are permitted, and only where this is done in the least rights-restrictive way.

However, this has increasingly come into conflict with evolving ideas of equality, in which the question is now asked: what can possibly justify encroachments on the principle of equality and non-discrimination? Of all justifications, that provided by religious freedom is the least acceptable. There is a new hierarchy of rights in which the right not to be discriminated against is at the pinnacle, and the right to manifest religious belief in practice and teaching is of far lesser importance. What vanishes in this kind of analysis is the right of organizations to select staff who will fit well with the mission and purpose of the organization. But the right to *select* is a positive right; the right to *discriminate* expresses the same idea in negative and pejorative terms.

Must the Pope be Catholic?

The insistence that the Pope should be Catholic involves discrimination against those who are not Catholic. Furthermore, the doctrine that only men may be ordained to the priesthood also discriminates against half the population who cannot meet this criterion, and so could never be Pope. It follows that the Catholic Church discriminates against a large majority of the world in its restrictive criteria for election as Pope. So, should the law intervene in the name of advancing human rights? The idea might seem preposterous, but for some people who place very little value on freedom of religion, there are few, if any, limits upon the scope of government regulation of religious bodies. Australian law professors Evans and Gaze wrote as long ago as 2008:

> There is an increasingly powerful movement to subject religions to the full scope of discrimination laws, with some scholars now suggesting that even core religious practices (such as the ordination of clergy) can be regulated in the name of equality.[27]

That doesn't sound all that different from the level of state control that the government had over clergy in communist Eastern Europe before the dismantling of the Iron Curtain (see the introduction),

27 C Evans and E Gaze, 'Between religious freedom and equality: Complexity and context', *Harvard International Law Journal*, 2008, 49:41.

or from the level of control governments assert in countries today where religious freedom is severely constrained.

For some, at least, 'human-rights principles' have become a new holy book for secular priests. In the eyes of some of the more extreme interpreters, these principles should take precedence over the holy book of a religion, even in terms of how the religion governs itself. The demand for one version of 'equality' displaces freedom—including freedom of belief as manifested in the life of religious communities. How far this intrusion of 'human-rights principles' into the self-ordering of religious communities will go remains to be seen. But we should not accept at face value any claim that in the modern world of human-rights analysis, all rights are treated equally.

5

FAITH PERSPECTIVES

How can we respond to the present times with Christian faith?

As Christians in Western countries, we are not used to the idea that the law might in certain respects be weaponized against us, or that the State might want to regulate what we do even within our organizations in ways that could clash with the precepts of our faith. We have been used to a legal system that developed in the soil of Christian nations. This is not to say that the law in Western countries has ever been 'Christian' as such. In continental Europe, by far the greatest influence on the development of the law was Roman law, rather than Christian ideas. However, in various ways, the law—both in the 'common law' countries and those in continental Europe—has given expression to Christian values, especially on such issues as sex and marriage.[1]

In the past, regrettably, the law has also been used to enforce some religious beliefs and church traditions at the expense of the religious freedom of others. Anyone who has studied the history of Europe in the 150 years after Martin Luther nailed his 95 theses to the door of the Castle Church in Wittenberg on 31 October 1517

---

1   'Common law' refers to a body of law developed through judicial decisions and precedents. Australia, Canada, New Zealand, the UK and the USA are all 'common law' countries. The main alternative is 'civil law', which means reliance on comprehensive laws being codified by legislators.

will know that much bloodshed followed. Those who embraced new Protestant understandings of the faith did so at great risk to their freedom, and even to their lives, in countries that remained loyal to the Pope. Conversely, Catholics who did not share the views of a ruling Protestant majority found their religious liberty suppressed. Even in the Geneva of Calvin's time, which was largely a sanctuary for religious liberty, Michael Servetus was sentenced to be burned at the stake for heresy.[2] The Zurich of Zwingli's time persecuted the Anabaptists in their midst. Indeed, the Anabaptists were persecuted everywhere. As one historian succinctly put it: "Protestants beheaded or drowned Anabaptists, Catholics burned them alive".[3] Religious tolerance was not one of the great virtues of the 16th century anywhere in Europe.

However, for most of the past 150 years in Anglophone countries at least, the law has supported the religious freedom of people of all faiths. What is becoming increasingly clear is that in many countries, the tide is now going out on the religious freedom we have hitherto enjoyed. There are various reasons for this.

Why the hostility from so many towards faith?

Religious freedom is gradually being curtailed to the extent that it is perceived as imposing upon the rights of others. In particular, the freedoms associated with religious freedom—especially freedoms of speech and conscience—are increasingly seen as having the potential to impact on others. This includes all public religious teaching, even sermons.

Why should the things taught from a pulpit have an impact upon others who are not there to hear it and have no connection of any kind with those who do hear it? Years ago, we might have said there could not possibly be any such harm. However, views have shifted.

---

2   See J Witte Jr, *The Reformation of Rights: Law, Religion and Human Rights in Early Modern Calvinism*, Cambridge University Press, 2008, pp 67–70.

3   M Kottelin-Longley, "'What shall I do? The more I kill the greater becomes their number!": The suppression of Anabaptism in early sixteenth century', *Scripta Instituti Donneriani Aboensis*, 2006, 19:184 (journal.fi/scripta/article/view/67308).

When it comes to sensitive areas where religious faith may come into conflict with contemporary views, the very utterance of a sermon may itself be perceived as an attack on the dignity of those whose lives or choices are called into question.

Perhaps this explains the extreme reactions of the leadership at Trent College to Bernard Randall's very mild sermon encouraging students to think for themselves on such issues as same-sex marriage and whether people can change sex (see chapter 3). As his opponents saw it, even uttering such a view was to do harm to students with a minority sexual orientation or gender identity. To do so from the authority of the pulpit must have seemed to the school leadership to be unforgiveable.

While usually much more licence than this is given to what is said from the pulpit, when a Christian agency is working in a 'public-facing' role, its religious freedom to hold views or policies that might upset others may well be more constrained.

This kind of dynamic was at work in the case of *Catholic Care (Diocese of Leeds) v Charity Commission for England and Wales*,[4] when the Court upheld a decision by the Charity Tribunal not to allow a Catholic adoption agency to maintain its policy of only serving married couples. The reason the tribunal gave is that it would be 'particularly demeaning' to same-sex couples. On this view, the fact that same-sex couples could apply to adopt through another agency is beside the point. The fact that *any* agency limits the opportunity to adopt to heterosexual married couples is perceived as diminishing the dignity of a same-sex couple. On such a view, there is no room for arguing that it is generally best for children to be placed with adoptive parents of different sexes.

The moral imperative to eliminate discrimination wherever it is found explains much of the clash that has arisen between theologically conservative religious organizations and the perceived rights of those who are same-sex attracted or identify as transgender. This has led to campaigns to remove from anti-discrimination laws any exceptions that allow religious organizations to discriminate against those who identify as LGBTQ+.

4   [2010] 4 All ER 1041. See chapter 2.

A second reason for hostility towards Christians is because of our moral teachings. People want to believe that they can make unconstrained choices in an effort to maximize their personal happiness, free of any limitations or responsibilities towards others. Christian teaching, in myriad ways, stands against that proposition. Jesus taught us to love our neighbours as ourselves. He did not teach that our only responsibility is to love ourselves. The Gospels are full of his teaching on how we must live our lives with a concern for others. The apostle Paul urged Christians, "follow my example, as I follow the example of Christ" (1 Cor 11:1)—specifically in a willingness to lay aside personal rights for the sake of others (1 Cor 9:15–23).

One of the most difficult teachings for non-believers to accept is that there should be any constraints on sexual freedom, other than that the sex is consensual. Since the sexual revolution of the 1960s, fuelled by the availability of reasonably reliable pharmaceutical contraception for women, there has been a gradual relaxation of moral constraints on sex before or outside of marriage. Surveys indicate that disapproval of adultery remains quite high,[5] but for those who are not married, there are few if any constraints in secular culture.

In recent years there has been a backlash against unconstrained sexual freedom, with secular feminist writers pointing out how this leads to a culture in which men can pressure a young woman into sex that she really doesn't want, but that she feels obliged to accept so she is not out of step with the prevailing cultural norms.[6] However, there remains strong resistance to the idea that I should be allowed to disapprove of how you live or what choices you make with your body. The existence of a morality that disapproves of unconstrained sexual freedom is a quiet affront to those who do not share that morality, even if it is unspoken. This goes far beyond disapproval of same-sex relationships.

5   See M Vitiello, 'Rethinking adultery', *Criminal Justice Ethics*, 2017, 36(3):314–326 (tandfonline.com/doi/full/10.1080/0731129X.2018.1424758). 90 per cent of Americans disapprove of adultery, up from 70 per cent in 1970.
6   See, for example, L Perry, *The Case Against the Sexual Revolution: A new guide to sex in the 21st century* (Polity, 2022).

Hostility to Christian teaching on sex and marriage is not new, of course. This is William Blake's famous poem, 'The Garden of Love', written in 1794:

I went to the Garden of Love,
And saw what I never had seen:
A Chapel was built in the midst,
Where I used to play on the green.

And the gates of this Chapel were shut,
And 'Thou shalt not' writ over the door;
So I turn'd to the Garden of Love,
That so many sweet flowers bore.

And I saw it was filled with graves,
And tomb-stones where flowers should be:
And Priests in black gowns, were walking their rounds,
And binding with briars, my joys & desires.

For the non-Christian, Christian moral rules may be perceived as "binding with briars" their joys and desires, particularly where the rhetorical emphasis has been on denouncing consensual sexual relations outside marriage as sinful.

It is not only in the area of sex that the secular emphasis on 'living your best life', despite collateral damage to others, conflicts with Christian teaching. Divorce is another area where the secular values of the day do not allow for disapproval of someone's choice to leave their marriage in order to pursue greater personal fulfilment, despite the harm this may cause to their partner or to children. "I hate divorce", said the Lord through the prophet Malachi (Mal 2:16, NASB). To the secular mind, such hatred of a personal lifestyle choice is both incomprehensible and offensive.

This explains a lot of the vehement opposition to public expressions of traditional Christian teaching. Julian Porteous, the Catholic Archbishop who was dragged before an anti-discrimination tribunal for distributing a booklet explaining his Church's opposition to same-sex marriage in 2015 (see chapter 3), experienced further trouble in 2024 for a mild pastoral letter distributed to parents in

Catholic schools.[7] In it, he explained that the Church believes in the notion of truth, and of an objective moral law. Abortion and euthanasia, he said, are opposed to that moral law. He went on to say that efforts to disconnect gender from biological sex deny the reality of who we are as God created us—male and female. Furthermore, God created male and female to be sexually complementary and to be united in marriage, which the Church regards as indissoluble. He went on to say that living together outside of marriage is wrong.

No-one ought to have been particularly surprised by a Catholic Archbishop articulating these rather fundamental doctrines of his Church. Yet, he lamented: "It is not impossible in the coming years that the very expression of Catholic belief on certain matters could essentially be made illegal." As if right on cue, the Archbishop's pastoral letter was vigorously denounced by advocacy groups and politicians, two of whom claimed that the circulation of the pastoral letter, in itself, breached anti-discrimination laws.[8] It was homophobic and transphobic, said critics, and contained "misinformation", "disinformation" and "hateful speech".[9] The Archbishop seems to have been correct that there were politicians in his community who would like to make the promulgation of Catholic teaching on these issues illegal. His offence was not that he holds the beliefs that his Church has for so long taught; even the most radical activists will allow him that freedom of belief. His offence was that he dared to promulgate these teachings to parents who have chosen to send their children to Catholic schools.

A third reason for hostility to Christianity—but not to other religions such as Islam or Hinduism—is the role it has played in the development of Western civilization. Christianity to the West is like

7   J Porteous, 'We are salt to the earth: Pastoral letter', 2 May 2024 (calameo.com/read/002628780aa0396aa14cc).

8   C Balen, 'Catholic archbishop's denouncement of "transgender lobby", legal abortion, euthanasia, same-sex marriage, heavily criticised', *ABC News*, 14 May 2024 (abc.net.au/news/2024-05-14/catholic-archbishop-julian-porteous-letter-to-parents-criticised/103838640).

9   'Tasmanian LGBTIQA+ advocates slam Archbishop's "homophobic misinformation" in school letter', *Pulse Tasmania*, 14 May 2024 (pulsetasmania.com.au/news/tasmanian-lgbtiqa-advocates-slam-archbishops-homophobic-misinformation-in-school-letter).

the womb to human life. While other influences, notably Greek philosophy and Roman civic order, have also played an important role in the Western tradition, Western civilization is incomprehensible without understanding the profound influence of Christianity. This is reflected in its core values, such as ideas of equality and individual human rights.[10] It is reflected in its art and music, much of which, prior to the 20th century, was profoundly religious. It is reflected in the architecture of cities, towns and villages, in which cathedrals and churches are often the most beautiful and prominent buildings.

It is no exaggeration to say that in many spheres of Western society, especially its universities and cultural centres, leading intellectuals hate the West and all it stands for, even as they benefit enormously from the society that Western values make possible. Movements opposed to racism and 'white supremacy', or promoting decolonization or queer theory, are undergirded by a belief that the Western world can be divided into oppressors and oppressed, and that every aspect of society can be understood with reference to a quest to gain or maintain power.

This hatred of the West can often involve very curious choices. When war broke out in the Middle East, following the brutal attack by Hamas on Israeli settlements near the border of Gaza on October 7, 2023, protests against Israel erupted all over the Western world. Many of the demonstrators identified with radical progressive politics. For them, Palestinians were the oppressed group. Israelis were the oppressors, notwithstanding the wholesale rape and murder that Israelis had experienced at the hands of Hamas in the October 7 attacks. One of the strangest protest groups was "Queers for Palestine",[11] members of which were filmed holding up placards at various rallies. Such an alliance looks incoherent, if it is not understood that this group sees itself as standing together against common oppressors—namely, those who hold power in the West. In the coalition of the marginalized, one oppressed group must stand in solidarity

10   J Locke, *Second Treatise on Civil Government*, 1690; L Siedentop, *Inventing the Individual: The Origins of Western Liberalism*, Allen Lane, 2014.
11   C Wilson, 'Queers for Palestine', *rs21*, 15 November 2023 (revsoc21.uk/2023/11/15/queers-for-palestine).

with another,[12] notwithstanding the harsh realities for openly 'queer' people in a country or area ruled by a conservative Islamic government such as Hamas.

For those who oppose the established system of societal governance, who want to 'deconstruct' or 'decolonize', opposition to Christianity is a necessary aspect of opposition to all that the West stands for. This is because Christianity is so closely associated with the established order of Western civilization. It is Christianity's huge contribution to modern Western society that is claimed as the justification for sustained opposition to the faith now. Whether people are opposed to patriarchy, or motivated by the rights of those who are same-sex attracted or 'gender diverse', or support decolonization, the church is seen as standing for what they find morally offensive. Christians who are open about their faith in the public square challenge the hegemony of politically progressive secular values. In this way, they represent a threat in a way that other religions do not.

Jesus' warnings about persecution

For the Christian who is familiar with the New Testament, none of this ought to come as a surprise. The contemporary reasons for hostility to the Christian faith and to those who profess it may be relatively new, but persecution is not. It dates back to our crucified Lord, who warned his nascent flock of the troubles that were to come. "If the world hates you", said Jesus, "keep in mind that it hated me first" (John 15:18). Jesus told his disciples:

> All this I have told you so that you will not fall away. They will put you out of the synagogue; in fact, the time is coming when anyone who kills you will think they are offering a service to God. They will do such things because they have not known the Father or me. I have told you this, so that when their time comes you will remember that I warned you about them. (John 16:1–4)

12 S Atshan, *Queer Palestine and the Empire of Critique*, Stanford University Press, 2020.

The apostle John provides an explanation for that persecution:

> This is the verdict: Light has come into the world, but people loved darkness instead of light because their deeds were evil. (John 3:19)

Knowing that his people would experience persecution throughout history, Jesus taught that we are to love our enemies and pray for those who persecute us (Matt 5:44).

The church, born in the dramatic events of Pentecost, was only a year or two old before it experienced serious persecution. The apostles were imprisoned together (Acts 5:17ff), as was Peter on another occasion (Acts 12:4ff). Stephen was stoned to death (Acts 7:54ff). James, brother of John, was also killed (Acts 12:2). Paul's extraordinary ministry was punctuated by long periods of incarceration as well as public beatings before he too was put to death. Tradition tells us that John was the only one of the apostles who lived into old age and died naturally.

Jesus' teaching on persecution, and his warnings to his own disciples about what they would experience, places the contemporary hostility towards Christianity into perspective. The reasons why there is so much hostility to Christianity, predominantly among 'progressive' university-educated people, reflect a particular moment in history. In other eras, there have been other factors driving the persecution of the church.

The new 'groupthink' and intolerance towards Christianity

Many Christians have lived and died in countries where governments are profoundly hostile to their faith. That has not, to date, been our experience in Western countries; but after centuries in which the Christian faith has been central to the life of the West, we now see a new era of secularism in which Christianity is, at best, tolerated. Many see it as a belief system that is opposed to their ambition for a different kind of society—one in which the old moral order and the old power structures are overthrown. Unlike Marx and Lenin, these new revolutionaries do not seem to have a clear vision for what that society will look like. They reject liberalism, with its tradition of tolerance and respect for people with different views, but it is not clear how those who stand with the 'oppressed' against the 'oppressors' would organize the world differently. If there are always oppressors, and discourse is all about power, it is unclear what changes would bring about a society in which there is no oppression. This is, at best, a dreamy egalitarianism.

In this new era of a post-liberal order, it will be increasingly difficult to be a Christian. This is for three main reasons. First, people in the new social-justice movement have very strong moral convictions in the rightness of their ideas, and that means that those who hold different ideas are, to that extent, immoral. Secondly, they seem to believe that the expression of those different ideas should not be tolerated. People who hold wrong ideas on matters of concern to the social-justice movement should be silenced or shouted down by any means available, or driven from their jobs. One consequence of this is a diminishing level of respect for conscientious objection. Third, this movement has an extraordinarily strong tendency to 'groupthink'. In a world where so many are lonely, it is especially important to maintain membership of the group, and that may mean going along with whatever the latest beliefs are, however strange or irrational they may be. There could be few stranger beliefs for university-educated people to hold than that maths is 'racist' or that biological sex is a 'social construct', but these kinds of belief have gained traction, and those who want to belong must embrace the new beliefs.

Because many of us, as Christians, find we cannot go along with this groupthink, there may be professions that are no longer open to us. We will experience increasing difficulties in our jobs and professional lives because our faith is inconsistent with the values of the secular society. Increasingly, leaders or regulators of professions allow us no right of conscientious objection apart from long-established grounds, such as opposition to participation in an abortion procedure. Even some of these long-established protections are under threat. We must still trust to the sovereignty and love of God in our lives, but the losses and difficulties may not be easy for us to handle.

The example of Andrew Thorburn in Australia is illustrative of the kinds of problem that Christians in the public eye may encounter. Thorburn had been a business leader of great distinction, rising to be CEO of one of Australia's largest banks, although his tenure at the helm of the bank was the subject of criticism by a royal commission into the banking industry. After his time as a CEO came to an end, he was asked to take on the role of running an Australian Rules football team, Essendon. He had supported the team since he was a child.

But only a matter of hours after his appointment was announced, a social-media campaign was calling for Essendon to revoke his appointment. Why? Because Thorburn also chaired the Board of a thriving evangelical Anglican church, City on a Hill in Melbourne. Activists soon discovered recordings of sermons preached by church leaders who expressed opposition to abortion and spoke negatively of homosexual practice. These sermons were from a time before Thorburn joined this church community, but that didn't matter. Nor did it matter that he had led a large and successful corporation that had a demonstrated commitment to equality and non-discrimination. There was not even direct evidence that he held the same beliefs as the preachers whose views the activists so loudly condemned. It was guilt by association. Within a few hours, the then Premier of Victoria, Daniel Andrews, joined in the pile-on.[13]

Less than 24 hours after the appointment was announced, the Board indicated that Thorburn must choose between being club CEO or chairing the Board of his church. The club President said, "Essendon is committed to providing an inclusive, diverse and safe club, where everyone is welcome and respected".[14] The Board made clear that, despite these not being views that Andrew Thorburn had expressed personally and that were also made prior to him taking

13 'Daniel Andrews chastises Essendon Bombers over church "firestorm"', *The Daily Telegraph*, 4 October 2022 (dailytelegraph.com.au/sport/afl/daniel-andrews-chastises-essendon-bombers-church-firestorm/news-story/19232d84bc77319eb eabc8cdd96cdbb0).

14 Essendon Football Club, 'Statement on behalf of Dave Barham', *Essendon FC*, 4 October 2022 (essendonfc.com.au/news/1233305/statement-on-behalf-of-dave-braham).

up his role as chairman, he couldn't continue to serve in his dual roles at Essendon and City on the Hill.

Clearly, the club's commitment to being inclusive, diverse and welcoming didn't extend to the inclusion of evangelical Christians. Faced with a choice of resigning his church role or resigning from his new position at the football club, Thorburn chose to keep faith with his God and with the community of believers with whom he shared fellowship. The entire case demonstrates the contingent nature of the societal commitment to diversity and inclusion.

Cancel culture

While such public incidents of discrimination are unsettling, as are the many other instances of less-prominent Christian people losing their jobs because of their beliefs, it is important to emphasize that such instances are still uncommon. Most ordinary people in Western countries are very accepting of Christians, as they are of people of other faiths or ethnicities. Many people in positions of prominence in government, business, education and the major professions are likewise very tolerant, and hold to traditional liberal values of equality and non-discrimination.

However, some leaders use their positions of power and influence to advance particular social agendas that may make life difficult for Christians in the organization. Many others are cowed by the vehemence of activist groups campaigning for the organization not to tolerate beliefs that are incompatible with the values they espouse.

Christians in public life may find themselves subject to campaigns to 'cancel' them. Sometimes those campaigns are successful. Very often they are not, but those stories are not so often told. In the introduction, I mentioned my personal experience of discrimination at the University of Sydney. Many years later, in 2018, I was appointed Dean of Law at the University of Queensland. Within hours of the announcement, activists mobilized. A group of student leaders went to see the Vice-Chancellor, asking him to revoke the appointment because, in my role as a family law expert, I had written an argument against legalizing same-sex marriage.

It was reported to me that the Vice-Chancellor's response to the student leaders was robust. He told the students that the university had done its due diligence, and that it knew of my faith and the positions I had espoused in public life. He stood by the appointment committee's choice. As a university leader, he was committed to an understanding of 'diversity and inclusion' that included viewpoint diversity. The university leadership continued to take that robust position throughout my time there, ignoring a couple of 'hit pieces' in prominent newspapers.

However, the commitment of that university to viewpoint diversity and academic freedom is not as common as it should be; and there are numerous examples, in North America especially, of cancellation campaigns against university professors or lecturers that have been successful, resulting in their dismissal or forced resignation. Tyler VanderWeele, a devout Catholic professor of public health at Harvard, has given a detailed account of his own experience of being pursued because of views he had expressed on same-sex marriage and abortion.[15] Those views, Harvard's academic leadership acknowledged, fell within the bounds of his academic freedom. Nonetheless, they organized no fewer than 14 two-hour 'listening sessions' with students who expressed being deeply upset that someone who argued against same-sex marriage could be teaching in the School. Some called for him to be fired. Emails from academic leaders in the School referred to his views as "reprehensible", and being such as to "cause deep hurt, undermine the culture of belonging, and make other members of the community feel less free and less safe". Reflecting on the tumultuous events of that time, Professor VanderWeele observed:

> Although the administration acknowledged that my opinions were protected by freedom of expression and that I had not committed any academic misconduct, they seemed unwilling to formally communicate this to students, staff, or faculty ...

15 TJ VanderWeele, 'Moral controversies and academic public health: Notes on navigating and surviving academic freedom challenges', *Global Epidemiology*, 2023, 6 (doi.org/10.1016/j.gloepi.2023.100119).

The message that I felt was often being conveyed *to me* was that my views, while perhaps formally protected, should not in fact be present within academic public health.[16]

The great majority of Christians in Western societies will probably not experience these pressures in the workplace, because their faith is not directly relevant to the work they do, and because the expression of their faith does not arouse opposition from colleagues. However, any of us could experience issues of this kind, and it is very likely that in future decades more of us will do so. Increasingly, we will find our employment options more constrained than if we were not committed Christians. Many will be told that they are not allowed to "bring our whole selves to work". We must check our faith at the door—as if such a thing were possible for a follower of Jesus.

Facing the future without fear

This increasingly hostile environment will no doubt be challenging; but all such challenges are of benefit if they lead us to focus on what our faith teaches. We believe in the sovereignty of God and the love of God for each one of us. In the famous words of Romans 8, "neither death nor life, neither angels nor demons, neither the present nor the future, nor any powers, neither height nor depth, nor anything else in all creation, will be able to separate us from the love of God that is in Christ Jesus our Lord" (v 38).

God is sovereign. As Jesus taught us, the Father knows every hair on our head (Luke 12:7), and he loves us with a depth that is almost impossible to comprehend. Yet, as almost all of us experience at some time in our lives, his sovereignty and limitless power is not always exercised in a way that spares us from pain.

In Revelation 2–3, John records Jesus' letter to seven churches. To five of the seven, Jesus expresses criticisms of the congregation. To Laodicea, for example, he writes that they are "lukewarm" (Rev 3:16). Only two churches escape criticism. To the church in Philadelphia, Jesus' message was:

16   TJ VanderWeele, 'Moral controversies', pp 3–4 (emphasis original).

"Since you have kept my command to endure patiently, I will also keep you from the hour of trial that is going to come on the whole world to test the inhabitants of the earth." (Rev 3:10)

Conversely, to Smyrna, the message was:

"Do not be afraid of what you are about to suffer. I tell you, the devil will put some of you in prison to test you, and you will suffer persecution for ten days. Be faithful, even to the point of death, and I will give you life as your victor's crown." (Rev 2:10)

A tale of two churches, both faithful to God, yet with quite different experiences of God's hand upon their lives. We are guaranteed the eternal love and comfort of God. We are not guaranteed freedom from persecution. Even when we walk through the valley of the shadow of death, we should fear no evil, for our Shepherd is with us (Psalm 23).

The law: both a sword and a shield

In these increasingly difficult times, the law is sometimes a source of attack, and sometimes an important shield against attack. We may find ourselves subject to complaint under anti-discrimination or 'hate speech' laws, for no other reason than that we have expressed our understanding of Christian teaching. On the other hand, the law can be on the side of the Christian and provide remedies for wrongful treatment.

Andrew Thorburn's experience of being at the helm of Essendon football club for only 24 hours is illustrative of the point. The pile-on against Thorburn, merely for being involved in a church in which sermons had been preached with which people disagreed, was intense. The football club proudly asserted that it had certain values which were incompatible with what the church had been teaching. The club, it appeared, was on the right side of history, standing firm for abortion rights and against bigotry.

However, it was plain as daylight that the club was on the wrong side of the law. Thorburn was forced out of his newly announced role for no other reason than his religious faith. Eventually he reached a confidential settlement with Essendon, which issued a public apology. It really could have had no serious defence against a claim based upon religious discrimination.

Similarly, Harvard's Tyler VanderWeele had the law on his side. Indeed, one of his complaints about the way the Harvard administration handled the complaints against him is that they never made clear to the students calling for him to be fired that it would have been unlawful to dismiss him.[17]

There have been numerous instances in recent years of conference venues cancelling the bookings of Christian organizations because the event conflicts with their values, only to later find that they had to pay significant compensation as a result. A conference organized by British group Christian Concern in 2012 illustrates the issue. The event was entitled 'One Man, One Woman: Making the case for marriage for the good of society', and was planned in opposition to government moves to legalize same-sex marriage. It was originally booked to be held at the headquarters of the Law Society in London in May 2012.[18] However, that booking was cancelled only a couple of weeks before the event was due to take place. The Chief Executive of the Law Society issued a statement saying, "We are proud of our role in promoting diversity in the solicitors' profession and felt that the content of this conference sat uncomfortably with our stance".[19] The conference was then moved to the Queen Elizabeth II Conference Centre, a publicly owned building near the Houses of Parliament in Westminster. It cancelled the booking the day before the conference was due to take place, also citing its diversity policy.

Subsequently, both venues had to eat humble pie and settle with Christian Concern after legal action was taken. As part of that settlement, both the Law Society and the Conference Centre made statements expressing their support for freedom of speech and

17 TJ VanderWeele, 'Moral controversies', p 3.
18 The Law Society is the peak body for solicitors in England.
19 Iona Institute, 'Marriage conference cancelled for "diversity" reasons', *Iona Institute for Religion and Society*, 16 May 2012 (ionainstitute.ie/marriage-conference-cancelled-for-diversity-reasons).

recognizing that people are entitled to hold different views on a subject like same-sex marriage. The Law Society announced it would organize a full debate on same-sex marriage in which a number of eminent speakers would participate, including a speaker from Christian Concern.[20] The Queen Elizabeth II Conference Centre likewise said it would be happy to work closely with Christian Concern to stage a future event about marriage or another issue of interest.[21] While the amount of damages was kept confidential (as is usual in all such cases), it may be assumed that damages were paid.

Of course, awards of damages and public apologies do not in themselves make up for the harm caused by discriminatory behaviour towards Christian groups that are guilty of 'wrongthink'. But they do offer a warning to organizations that believe they can ignore the law with impunity based upon their 'progressive' values and commitment to 'diversity'. It is surprising how even an organization with as much legal knowledge as the Law Society can confuse public adulation with what is legal.

In the next chapter, we consider what the Christian's view of the law should be in the modern era, given that it may be both friend and foe to people of faith.

---

20 'Christian Concern and Law Society reach agreement over marriage conference cancellation', *Christian Concern*, 21 June 2013 (christianconcern.com/ccpressreleases/christian-concern-and-law-society-reach-agreement-over-marriage-conference-cancellation).

21 'Settlement reached over cancellation of Christian Concern's marriage conference', *Christian Concern*, 21 January 2015 (christianconcern.com/news/settlement-reached-over-cancellation-of-christian-concerns-marriage-conference).

PART II
LAW AND FAITH

6

THE LIMITATIONS ON OBEDIENCE TO GOVERNMENT

How, as Christians, do we balance obedience to God with obedience to divinely authorized government?

The growing intolerance towards religious belief, and the weaponization of the law against people of faith, raises what for many of us will be new questions about how we respond to laws that restrict our religious freedom. What, in general terms, should be the Christian's attitude to law? And what, in particular, should be our attitude to those laws that unreasonably restrict religious freedom? When, if at all, is it right to disobey the law?

Obedience to the law in the teachings of Jesus

Jesus lived in Israel in a time when the possibility of rebellion against the Roman government of the day was rarely very far beneath the surface. The Jewish people were, at all times, reluctant subjects of a foreign power. They looked back to days of glory under King David, when the twelve tribes of Israel were united under one leader, had the respect of the nations around them, and most importantly, were autonomous. Since that time, successive empires had ruled over their lands; but still many people looked to a Messiah who would be a deliverer of the Jewish people from the oppression of foreign rule.

Jesus gave no support to such aspirations. When asked directly about whether Jewish people should pay taxes, he replied that they should "give back to Caesar what is Caesar's, and to God what is God's" (Matt 22:21; see also Matt 17:24–27). When, in the Garden of Gethsemane, Peter took out his sword and cut off the ear of one of those sent to arrest Jesus, Jesus rebuked Peter for resorting to violence and healed the man's ear (John 18:10–11; Luke 22:50–51).

Jesus was not interested in political power; that was one of the temptations that the devil put before him in the Judean wilderness, but he rejected it (Matt 4:8–10; see also John 6:15). In his trials in Jerusalem, first before the Sanhedrin and then before Pilate, he did not challenge their authority to rule or to administer punishment. His kingdom was not of this world (John 18:36), and he sought to dissuade his disciples from looking for a Messiah who would liberate them from the Romans.

However, when it came to religious laws, Jesus had a nuanced approach. He was severely critical of the legalists who concerned themselves with obedience to minutiae while missing the big picture of how we should live in a way that honours God and cares for others (see, for example, Matthew 23:23–24). Generally, he obeyed the requirement to do no work on the Sabbath, but that did not stop him healing on such a day (John 7:23). The Gospels record several examples where religious leaders challenged him about his failure to obey the law as they understood it (see, for example, Matt 12:1–13).

Paul's teaching: God's good purpose for government

Paul had much more to say than Jesus about the role of government. Most well-known perhaps is his exposition of the nature of government in Romans 13. Government, he said, is given to us by God and has authority from God to "bear the sword" and "bring punishment on the wrongdoer" (v 4). Obedience to law is required, he instructs, not only because of possible punishment, but also "as a matter of conscience" (v 5). In a similar vein, Paul urged Titus to "remind the people to be subject to rulers and authorities, to be obedient, to be ready to do whatever is good" (Titus 3:1). In his first letter to Timothy,

Paul instructed believers to pray and give thanks for kings and all those in authority, that we might live quiet and godly lives and be free to preach the gospel (1 Tim 2:1–2).

Paul was not saying that any particular elected government is ordained by God. In democratic societies, sooner or later, governments change. In a two-party system, the red team and the blue team alternate every few years. In many democracies, multiple parties must seek to work in coalition to form a government. As a consequence, the composition of a government may go through frequent changes. All governments are ordained by God in the Romans 13 sense, even though who runs the government may change every few years, and policies might differ markedly from one government to the next.

There is no contradiction between submitting to government while also wanting to overthrow the government of the day at the ballot box. Romans 13 is not telling us that God is involved at the granular level of party politics. Paul's is a much more general and abstract claim— that government itself is a good that comes from God, whatever its inadequacies in any particular time and place. In modern societies, the vast apparatus of government continues to operate regardless of who is in power at any given time. Even during times of political uncertainty or when power is being handed over to a new government following an election, taxes continue to be collected, welfare payments continue to be made, public hospitals continue to operate, the police are still on the streets, and courts continue to do their work.

To understand what Paul is saying about government, it is only necessary to imagine what life would be like in a society where government has collapsed. Americans have had glimpses of this in recent years. After the death of George Floyd in Minneapolis in 2020, riots erupted all over the country. In many places, for a time at least, the police lost control of the streets. Shops were looted or burnt down.[1] In Seattle, activists even created a no-go area where police were not welcome, known as the Capitol Hill Autonomous Zone. In an effort to de-escalate the situation, the police chose to

---

1   D Taylor, 'George Floyd protests: A timeline', *New York Times*, 5 November 2021 (nytimes.com/article/george-floyd-protests-timeline.html).

withdraw from their police station in the neighbourhood. This lasted for several weeks, with crime in the area escalating as the community became essentially lawless.[2]

In explaining the role that God has given to government, Paul places a particular emphasis on its role in punishing crime. "Rulers", he wrote, "are God's servants, agents of wrath to bring punishment on the wrongdoer" (Rom 13:4). Modern criminologists tell us that the causes of crime are complex—that those who embark upon criminal activity are often themselves victims of severe disadvantage, or have had adverse childhood experiences.[3] True as that may be in many cases, no society can survive and flourish for long if crime has no consequences. If theft goes unpunished, property rights are undermined. If sexual assault goes unpunished, women and children in particular are exposed to considerable risk of harm. In many cases, mitigating circumstances should be considered in sentencing, and there is much room for argument about the methods and purposes of punishment. But few of us would like to live in a crime-ridden society where law and order has broken down. When this occurs, it is the poorest and most vulnerable in the society who suffer the most—those who cannot afford to move to a safer area or to insure the property they own.

The idea that government is God-given may be easier to accept in a modern and stable democratic society than in countries where government is oppressive, corrupt, or both (as it is in so many parts of the world). Yet even in these countries, the normal business of government and law enforcement carries on. It is generally better to be in a country with a harsh, undemocratic or oppressive government, than no working government at all. Augustine of Hippo expressed the issue when he described kingdoms without justice as "robber-bands enlarged".[4] As we discussed in chapter 1, even Hitler's

---

2   B Holden, 'Capitol Hill Autonomous Zone (CHAZ) or Organized Protest (CHOP) (Seattle)', *HistoryLink.org*, 30 December 2023 (historylink.org/File/22870).

3   For an introduction, see D Weatherburn, 'What Causes Crime?', NSW Bureau of Crime Statistics and Research, February 2001 (bocsar.nsw.gov.au/research-evaluations/2001/cjb54-what-causes-crime.html).

4   Augustine, *City of God Against the Pagans*, book 19, chapter 13.

government in Nazi Germany provided a measure of law and order. In ordinary ways, for ordinary people, the legal system in Nazi Germany operated to govern the society and to resolve disputes, much as it did prior to Hitler's ascension.

It is in this sense that government is from God; and for the most part, Roman law and government was good. It provided a stable and well-ordered society. Indeed, Roman law has since formed the basis for much of the law of modern Europe.

The paradox: God-given persecution?

However, Paul would also have been aware of the capacity of Roman law and government to be a source of persecution for Christians. Jesus himself was put to death on the authority of a Roman governor, despite having lived a sinless life. Paul suffered much in the course of his ministry (see, for example, 2 Cor 11:23–27), spending long periods of time in prison or under house arrest. His persecutors were, at different times, both the Jewish and Roman authorities.

The early church also experienced very severe persecution from the time when Stephen was stoned to death onwards (Acts 7:54–60). Some time after Paul wrote Romans, another wave of persecution occurred at the instigation of the Emperor Nero. He blamed the Christians for a fire in Rome in AD 64 that damaged or destroyed more than 70 per cent of the city. According to the Roman historian Tacitus, many Christians were put to death during this time in ways which demonstrated enormous cruelty:

> An immense multitude was convicted, not so much of the crime of firing the city, as of hatred against mankind. Mockery of every sort was added to their deaths. Covered with the skins of beasts, they were torn by dogs and perished, or were nailed to crosses, or were doomed to the flames and burnt, to serve as a nightly illumination, when daylight had expired.[5]

---

5   Tacitus, *The Annals of Imperial Rome*, book 25, chapter 44 in Church and Brodribb (eds), *Complete Works of Tacitus*, Random House, 1942.

It is believed that Paul was put to death during this persecution.[6]

Given this history, Romans 13 is all the more remarkable. It stands as an instruction for believers to respect the authority of government in spite of the persecution they experienced at its hands.

Peter's teaching in his first letter is consistent with that of Paul. In this letter, he was writing to a church that was now experiencing persecution. Yet he could write:

> Submit yourselves for the Lord's sake to every human authority: whether to the emperor, as the supreme authority, or to governors, who are sent by him to punish those who do wrong and to commend those who do right ... Show proper respect to everyone, love the family of believers, fear God, honour the emperor. (1 Pet 2:13–14, 17)

Later in the letter, he addressed the believers' experience of persecution at the hands of the Roman government, telling them to suffer for what is right, not for what is wrong: "If you suffer as a Christian, do not be ashamed, but praise God that you bear that name" (1 Pet 4:16). Peter, who had twice been imprisoned while in Jerusalem and was rescued on both occasions by angels (Acts 5:18ff, 12:4ff), knew full well that the law could be applied in ways that were unjust and oppressive. However, he did not teach disrespect for government or disobedience to government in general terms. If believers were to suffer punishment at the hands of government, it must be because they have been doing what is right in the eyes of God.

However, neither Paul nor Peter give us any reason to think that when governments persecute Christians or oppress the church, they are in any way doing God's work. Jesus taught us to pray, "deliver us from evil" (Matt 6:13, ESV).[7] When governments act in evil ways, they do not do so with God's authority or blessing.

---

6   'How did St. Paul the Apostle die?', *Brittanica.com* (britannica.com/question/ How-did-St-Paul-the-Apostle-die).

7   This could, alternatively, be translated "deliver us from the evil one" (NIV). But governments may be a means through which the evil one can attack Christians, so arguably the difference in translation is immaterial for our purposes.

Godly disobedience

While the default position for Christians is that we should be law-abiding citizens, submitting to governmental authority and praying for political leaders, there are limits to our obedience. A key New Testament passage on this issue is Acts 5. The apostles were arrested and put in jail after performing many signs and wonders among the people, leading many people to faith in Christ. After being rescued from prison by an angel, they immediately returned to preaching publicly in the temple courts, despite the authorities having commanded them "not to speak or teach at all in the name of Jesus" (Acts 4:18). The apostles were made to appear before the Sanhedrin again to be questioned by the high priest.

> "We gave you strict orders not to teach in this name," [the high priest] said. "Yet you have filled Jerusalem with your teaching and are determined to make us guilty of this man's blood" Peter and the other apostles replied: "We must obey God rather than human beings!" (Acts 5:28–29)

They went on to speak boldly of Jesus' resurrection.

In many countries of the world today, evangelism is forbidden. Christians are no more obliged to obey such laws now than Peter and John were in first-century Jerusalem. We pray for kings and all those in authority that we may be able to live peaceful and quiet lives and share the gospel with others (1 Tim 2:1–4). Where governments do not allow us this freedom, we are bound to obey our higher calling from the Lord. How we share the faith in such a context is another matter, and requires wisdom and discernment. But continuing to proclaim the lordship of the risen Christ is non-negotiable.

Governments may not even allow believers the freedom to meet together. As the Catholic underground movement experienced in Slovakia when I was there in the early 1980s,[8] even meeting in Bible-study groups carried great risk. The secret police were active in trying to uncover these groups, so the Slovak believers took great precautions. The instructions about how to get to each weekly

8　See the introduction.

meeting were only revealed a couple of days beforehand, so that if there was any breach of security, the fallout could be contained. Typically, the instruction was to meet at a particular bus or tram stop at a certain time, with further information being given from there. Despite the risks, the students followed the biblical injunction not to neglect meeting together—and in so doing they provided great encouragement and support for one another, and were able to "spur one another on toward love and good deeds" (Heb 10:24–25).

The command to submit to governing authorities in Romans 13 and elsewhere cannot properly be understood unless it is balanced with the recognition that it is sometimes right to disobey the law or not to comply with an instruction from rulers (which in Paul's time meant much the same thing). As Christians, we can usually live law-abiding lives and act as good citizens in the communities to which we belong; but we draw lines at the point that the government requires us to do what God clearly says we must not, or where the government says we must not do what God clearly says we should do. In situations where the church is being persecuted or severely restricted, Christians may need to break a country's laws in order to provide support for the persecuted believers—for example, by smuggling in Bibles or Christian books.

Daniel and his friends offer an example both of godly disobedience and great courage. Daniel had already stood upon his principles as a young man, being prepared for service in the Babylonian empire. He refused the fine foods that he was being served, eating only vegetables (Dan 1:6–16).

Later, as one of the three most senior officials in the empire, he faced a much greater challenge. His rivals set a trap, persuading King Nebuchadnezzar to issue an unalterable decree that anyone who prays to any god or human being, except the king, should be thrown into the lions' den (Dan 6:3–9). Daniel was not cowed by this. He continued to pray three times per day in front of an open window that looked out in the direction of Jerusalem. He took no steps to hide his practice; he was not prepared to be a secret believer.

Consequently, as is well known, he was thrown into the lion's den. He should have been torn to pieces within minutes, yet God sent his angel to shut the mouths of the lions, because Daniel was innocent of any wrongdoing towards the king. He had, of course, broken the law that forbade him to pray to his God. Daniel was saved, not *from* the lions' den, but *in* the lions' den (Dan 6:16–23).

Shadrach, Meshach and Abednego had a similar experience. Like Daniel, they were targeted by rivals for influence because of their faith. A law went out that everyone had to bow down and worship an image of gold that Nebuchadnezzar had set up. Whoever did not do so would be immediately thrown into a blazing furnace. The three men did not bow down, and their rivals accused them accordingly. A further charge was that they refused to worship the king's gods.

The response of the three men reflects what faith demands in such circumstances. They responded to the king:

> "King Nebuchadnezzar, we do not need to defend ourselves before you in this matter. If we are thrown into the blazing furnace, the God we serve is able to deliver us from it, and he will deliver us from Your Majesty's hand. But even if he does not, we want you to know, Your Majesty, that we will not serve your gods or worship the image of gold you have set up." (Dan 3:16–18)

As was Daniel's experience, God rescued them: they were not saved *from* the flames, but *in* the flames. The furnace was made so hot that it killed the soldiers guarding them, yet they were unharmed (Dan 3:19–27).

Shadrach, Meshach and Abednego had to take the risk of disobeying the law. They could have had no guarantee they would survive the blazing furnace. They had to take the step they did, trusting in a God who may not rescue them. Likewise, Queen Esther, at another time, had to take the risk of death in going uninvited to the king in order to plead for her people (Esth 4:9–16). God does not always spare us from trials; he may or may not rescue us when we are in the midst of them. We take the risk of obedience, no matter the cost.

Obeying a higher law

Ever since New Testament days, the Church has held in tension the duty to obey rulers with a recognition of the limits of their God-given authority. One way in which the church's greatest intellectual leaders have managed that tension has been by reference to the idea of 'natural law'. This refers to the notion that while governments enact human laws, there is a higher law to be found in the God-given natural order.

Such an idea went back to Aristotle (384–322 BC), who considered that everything contained an essential purpose. For Aristotle, the family was an association established by nature, and so was the state, since the result of human association is the community of the state. Aristotle concluded from these observations that "man is by nature a being inclined to a civic existence".[9]

These ideas were taken up by Roman writers and thinkers, especially the great advocate and statesman Cicero (106–43 BC) who, drawing his ideas from Stoic philosophy, argued that there were natural laws for the conduct of individuals, and that reason could discern these precepts. For Cicero, natural laws did not depend for their validity and status on any human authority recording them as law; these were the elemental principles of justice that ought to be universal.

Paul also accepted these ideas. He argued that there was a natural law that was not merely discoverable by reason, but was, in a manner of speaking, 'intuitive'—written on people's hearts, with the conscience bearing witness to it (Rom 2:14–15). Of course, he also made clear that reason alone could not bring us to a knowledge of Christ's saving work (1 Cor 1:18–25).

In the teaching of the early Church Fathers, natural-law teaching gained another interpretation. They posited the idea of a fall from a perfect, or 'natural', order, along with the loss of an age of innocence. Augustine argued that humankind, as originally created by God, was

---

9   Aristotle, *Politics*, book 1, chapter 2. This is literally translated, "man is by nature a political animal". However, this rendering has attained a different colloquial meaning and may be misunderstood.

not intended to be subject to the oppression of government nor to be enslaved.[10] Such institutions were the result of the fall from that original created order.

The idea that there was a natural law that was higher than human laws provided the basis for Christian thinking about disobedience to the laws of a given State, ruler or government. Origen, a great theologian from the middle of the third century, wrote that:

> Where the law of nature, that is of God, enjoins precepts contradictory to the written laws, consider whether reason does not compel a man to dismiss the written code and the intention of the lawgivers far from his mind, and to devote himself to the divine Lawgiver and to choose to live according to His word, even if in doing this he must endure dangers and countless troubles and death and shame.[11]

This idea was taken up in the writings of Thomas Aquinas (1225–1274), an Italian Dominican friar who taught at the University of Paris. Aquinas was responsible for a systematic exploration of philosophy and theology that profoundly affected thinking in the Western world for centuries thereafter. In Aquinas' view, on the one hand, God gives temporal authority; but on the other hand, rulers govern in order to direct people towards their own good or to the common good.

Aquinas answered the question of when human laws ought to be obeyed by stating that a law is just, and therefore binding in conscience, when it is ordered for the common good, and thus consistent with natural law. He wrote: "Every law laid down by men has the force of law in that it flows from natural law. If on any head, it is at variance with natural law, it will not be law, but spoilt law."[12] The commands of unjust laws did not need to be obeyed, he said, except to avoid scandal or riot.[13]

In other words, Aquinas allowed for the possibility that unjust

---

10 Augustine, *City of God*, book 19, chapter 15.
11 Origen, *Contra Celsum*, book 5, chapter 37.
12 Aquinas, *Summa Theologica*, 1–2, question 95, article 2.
13 Aquinas, *Summa Theologica*, 1–2, question 96, article 4.

laws might need to be disobeyed. But he added several caveats to this proposition. Sometimes unjust laws need to be obeyed because it would injure the Christian's reputation to do otherwise, or because it avoids civil strife. Sometimes, we are not to insist upon our rights. However, Aquinas was clear that a law which is contrary to divine law—such as a law commanding idolatry—should never be obeyed.

What God gives, God can take away

Paul's teaching that God gives government for our good contains within it an implicit limitation on the authority of government. As Michael Jensen explains, rulers "have their power from God, and he can take it from them, just as he gives it. The authority of earthly rulers is subsidiary to the authority of God."[14]

That idea has been fundamental to Christian thought about government through the centuries, and has indeed provided the theological basis for working to overthrow a government if the circumstances demand it. The great Spanish bishop and legal thinker Isidore of Seville, who lived between about 560–636 AD, wrote that "kings can retain their power only if they govern with rectitude, otherwise they are doomed to lose it".[15]

Over time, the notion of "rectitude" came to be understood as imposing an obligation on the monarch to act in the best interests of the governed. Towards the end of the 11th century, a German monk named Manegold of Lautenbach expressed the relationship between government and governed as a form of contract. He said that although the ruler's authority was given by God, the ruler owed obligations to govern justly. It followed from this that if the ruler broke his agreement by disrupting the things that he was appointed to keep in order, the people were released from their obligation of obedience.[16]

14 MP Jensen, *Subjects and Citizens: The politics of the gospel: Lessons from Romans 12-15*, Matthias Media, 2024, p 91.
15 *The Etymologies of Isidore of Seville*, book 1, chapter 29, section 3; *Sententiae*, book 3, chapter 48, section 7.
16 JM Kelly, *A Short History of Western Legal Theory*, Clarendon Press, 1992, p 98.

John of Salisbury, an influential political theorist, offered a similar argument. In his work *Policraticus* (1159), he said that, on the one hand, kings hold office by God's will. Even tyrants do so, since they are means by which God chastens his people. But oppressive rulers would eventually be overthrown. At the same time, John also affirmed the right—and even the duty—of civil disobedience. No ruler could be justified in commanding a subject to disobey precepts of the Christian faith, and those who did so should not be obeyed. John even went as far as to say that subjects might need to uphold the law by killing tyrants who violated it.[17]

Of course, killing a tyrannical ruler is the most extreme action a Christian could take. David did not consider it right to kill King Saul, even when he had ample opportunity to do so. He felt it was wrong to kill the Lord's anointed even though Saul was, at the time, hunting David—no doubt with a view to killing him (1 Sam 24:1–7).

Conversely, Dietrich Bonhoeffer, a leading German theologian and church leader who led religious opposition to Adolf Hitler, reached the conclusion that he was justified in joining a plot to kill Hitler. His qualms about doing so were not based upon the morality of the act, but its efficacy. That is, Bonhoeffer counselled that such an act should not be attempted unless the plotters could be confident that a better government would result.[18] In the end, the plot failed. Bonhoeffer was arrested, sentenced to death, and hanged not long before the Second World War ended.

While murdering a ruler is at the extreme of possible actions, there has been a consistent theme in Christian thought that there may be circumstances when it is right to depose a ruler—that is, to engage in a coup or revolution. Aquinas wrote:

> If it is a people's right to provide itself with a king, and if that king tyrannically abuses the royal power, there is no injustice if the community deposes or checks him whom they have raised

---

17 H Berman, *Law and Revolution: The Formation of the Western Legal Tradition*, Harvard University Press, 1985, pp 281–282.

18 E Metaxas, *Bonhoeffer: Pastor, Martyr, Prophet, Spy*, revised edn, Thomas Nelson, 2021, p 425.

to the kingship … because, by not faithfully conducting himself in government as the royal office demands, he has brought it on himself if his subjects renounce their bargain with him.[19]

Such ideas were echoed centuries later by the great political philosopher John Locke (1632–1704). Locke was a devout Christian who wrote what has been described as "the most influential work on natural law ever written":[20] his *Second Treatise on Civil Government* (1690). In this book, Locke put forward a theory that government exists to protect the natural rights of its citizens, rights which existed in the state of nature. His argument was based upon the fundamental premises that the natural order is ordained by God, that God has prescribed rules of conduct that were discoverable by reason and objectively valid, and that such rules can be known with certainty.[21] In Locke's view, therefore, civil government is based upon the consent of each individual to abide by the rules of the community. This is the social contract, which exists for the purpose that the natural rights of each individual should be better protected thereby. Government is necessary so that there is a common and independent arbiter of disputes, and so that each person's rights will be guarded and protected. Power is given to government as a form of trust for the benefit of the people.

It followed from Locke's ideas about the role of government that he should endorse the possibility of revolution—which he termed the "appeal to heaven"—when government fails to uphold those rights.[22]

When governments represent an existential threat

The issue of when not to obey government also arose in the aftermath of the Reformation. In his writings, Martin Luther held closely to Romans 13 and related New Testament passages. For him, monarchs and others in authority were God's vice-regents on earth,

---

19 Aquinas, *De Regimine Principum,* book 1, chapter 7.
20 PE Sigmund, *Natural Law in Political Thought,* University Press of America, 1971, p 81.
21 J Locke, *Essay Concerning Human Understanding*, chapter 2.
22 J Locke, *Second Treatise of Government*, chapter 14, section 168; chapter 16, section 176.

called to implement God's will and to enforce divine justice, if necessary by violence and capital punishment. The monarch was also the 'father of the community' who needed to care for his subjects as if they were his children.[23]

Luther himself didn't develop ideas about how then to respond to a ruler who failed to exemplify those characteristics. How, for example, should Lutherans respond if government represented an existential threat to the Reformation? This was a question that necessarily exercised the minds of his followers after his death, as they faced severe persecution from rulers seeking to re-establish papal authority and to crush the Lutheran 'heresy'.

In the Magdeburg Confession (1550), written four years after Luther's death, the leaders of the small Saxon city of Magdeburg sought to justify disobedience to the will of the Holy Roman Emperor, Charles V, who laid siege to the city. Charles sought, by force of law, to reimpose Catholic doctrines and liturgies on the people. John Witte Jr summarizes the arguments they advanced in responding to the biblical texts that seemed to require submission to the will of the Emperor:

> The Magdeburg confession first countered the many biblical texts that called faithful Christians to honour, respect and obey the emperor and other political authorities for the sake of conscience and the Gospel. Yes, the Confession argued, we must honour the authorities so that "our days may be long". But if our days are being cut short, then we should not honour those authorities who shorten them. Yes, political authorities were "appointed by God to do good". But if they are not doing good, then they could not have been appointed by God …Yes, we must "render to Caesar the things that are Caesar's and to God the things that are God's." But if Caesar wants or takes what is

23 See J Witte Jr, 'Resisting political authority to protect faith and morality: Enduring lessons from the Lutheran Reformation' in P Naude, M Welker and J Witte Jr (eds), *The Impact of Political Economy: on character formation, ethical education, and the communication of values in late modern pluralistic societies*, Evangelische Verlagsanstalt, 2023, pp 197–199.

God's, then we must withhold or retrieve it for God's sake. Yes, "he who resists the authorities resists God". But if the authorities resist God, then surely we must avenge God's honour.[24]

The Magdeburg Confession went on to argue that biblically, different spheres of authority rest in the church, the state and the family. None of these three spheres of authority should get mixed up with one another or intrude upon another's mandate, and none should violate the sovereignty of God. All authorities thus ruled conditionally on not abandoning, betraying or exceeding their mandate.[25]

This is an important issue in understanding the scope of Romans 13. In the Roman Empire of Paul's time, the government would never have believed that part of its work was to decide theological disputes internal to the life of the church or to resolve who should be appointed to the leadership of the church at Jerusalem or Ephesus. The government's role was to ensure law and order, defend the empire's borders, and have laws about matters such as property ownership and compensation for harm caused to others. Romans 13 does not indicate that God has given authority to governments to control every aspect of our churches and our family lives.

Obedience to law in a democratic society

Of course, Christians in Western societies are not in anything like the same position as the Lutherans of Magdeburg or countless other situations in the history of the church where the question of armed resistance or revolution has had to be seriously considered. These historical examples are of value mainly in showing how the great theologians and philosophers of the past grappled with the ideas of civil disobedience and how to reconcile submission to governmental authority with the need, at times, to oppose it.

We are in a quite different situation—one where there may be occasional laws that we cannot comply with, or are not sure that we can comply with. We may also face situations where governments

24   J Witte Jr, 'Resisting political authority', p 201.
25   J Witte Jr, 'Resisting political authority', pp 201–202.

overreach their authority and pass laws that fall outside of the authority that God's word gives to government.

In facing such situations, it is valuable to be reminded of those who have made a strong case *against* civil disobedience. It raises an important question: if we gain the benefits of living in a democratic society, should we not also bear the burdens? After all, we can vote; we can oppose the enactment of laws or seek to have them changed; we can participate in our democracy in many other ways. Should we not, then, respect the outcomes of democracy? For example, if the result of a change in understanding of what it means to be a multicultural society is that laws are passed diminishing religious freedom, should we not just accept the new limitations as the price of living in a society where such democratic participation is possible?

There is a strong case for saying that Christians owe obligations to the society to obey the law even when we disagree with it. Understanding the strength of that obligation is a necessary condition for appreciating the scope for non-compliance. In essence, the argument for obeying the laws of a democratic society, beyond the instructions in passages like Romans 13, is that the rule of law is fundamental to the success of Western democracies.

The rule of law is a restraint on the powers of government. It implies that a person may be punished for breaches of the law, and not for anything else. It implies also that the government will, itself, be subject to law. That is, it will act constitutionally and in accordance with the laws that the Parliament or legislature has passed.

This idea has a very long history, rooted in Christian thought. It has long been held, for example, that the ruler was bound to respect the people's laws that were antecedent to him. Thus Bracton's *Treatise on the Law and Customs of England*, a great 13th-century work, stated that the king had a duty to obey the law, since the king is under God and the law. Bracton argued in essence that it is not the king who makes the law (although he may add to the body of laws in his time), but the law that makes the king.[26]

---

26   H De Bracton, *On the Law and Customs of England* (S Thorne trans), Belknap Press, 1968.

The principle of submission to the law applies also to handing over power if defeated in an election. The ruler who is subject to law must refer any disputed results to the courts for adjudication. He or she will accept the court's verdict, whether favourable or unfavourable. Essential to the rule of law is that judges are independent. They will not be dictated to by a government official who indicates which way the court should determine the matter.

A strong commitment to the rule of law is also important to the economy. Foreign investors considering providing funds for a business venture want to be assured that the government will adhere to the laws that have been passed, and not seek substantial bribes to get planning permission or other permits. They will want to know that courts will adjudicate any contract dispute fairly.

While the rule of law is primarily about constraints upon the arbitrary power of government, this fundamental principle has implications for individual people, including Christians. If we benefit from a legal system in which we can have a reasonable expectation that government will obey the law, should not governments expect us to do so as well? We benefit from order and stability—should we not accept that it comes at a price?

The morality of civil disobedience

The great Greek philosopher Socrates certainly thought so. Socrates was unfairly sentenced to death in 399 BC for 'impiety' and allegedly 'corrupting the youth'. Most likely, his real crime was that he had offended the power brokers of the city.

By this time, Socrates was about 70 years old. He had several chances to avoid death. He could have fled the city to avoid a trial, living out the rest of his days elsewhere. Even after his conviction, he could have pleaded with the assembly to allow him to go into exile. He could also have allowed himself to be rescued from prison by his friends, as they had urged him to let them do. That would probably have involved bribing the guards. He could then have gone into exile in another city. There were many opportunities to escape an unjust punishment.

According to Plato's account in *Crito*, his friend Crito offered Socrates a last chance to escape on the eve of his scheduled death. In the dialogue recorded in this work, Socrates explained at length to Crito why he regarded it as ethically wrong to escape his sentence. The city-state of Athens had nurtured him, providing the context for his civic existence. He considered that obedience to the laws of the city-state in which he had lived was therefore an absolute obligation. To flout those laws, he said, would be to destroy them, and to renege upon his solemn agreement as a member of that community. In any event, he had a strong belief that there was a life after death, so his death would not be the end of his existence. His philosophy was that living should not be his priority. His priority should be living well—and that meant living *rightly*.

As Christians, we are not in quite the same place. Socrates' whole life was lived in the one world of Athens. Ours is lived in two worlds, for as our Lord said, we are "*in* the world" but not "*of* the world" (John 17:11, 14–16). We are citizens of two kingdoms. We have an unending and unshaken allegiance to God, whose call upon our lives may not be compatible with the laws of our city. Nonetheless, Socrates' arguments ring through the ages as a powerful case to respect the law, even at the cost of losing one's life from an unjust verdict. Jesus, of course, did the same: he too could have been rescued from death had the Father chosen that path (Luke 22:42). Yes, of course, there are essential differences between Jesus' death and that of anyone else: not only was he dying as the one true sacrifice for sin, but he was also the only completely innocent person ever to live. Yet it remains striking that, humanly speaking, God's chosen method for his Son to go to death was as the result of a corrupt, unjust legal verdict.

The great American political philosopher John Rawls (1921–2002), a key thinker in the liberal tradition, also grappled with the problem of civil disobedience. He distinguished between conscientious refusal—when someone decides they can't comply with a law—and civil disobedience. Conscientious refusal, he said, "is not necessarily based on political principles; it may be founded on religious or other principles at variance with the constitutional order".[27] By way of contrast, civil disobedience—which he defined as a public, nonviolent, conscientious yet political act contrary to law, with the aim of bringing about change—is an appeal to a commonly shared conception of justice.[28]

Civil disobedience, in Rawls' view, had to be done in public in order to be an appeal to shared community values about justice. It was justified not by self-interest, but by a concern for the public good. Civil disobedience did not mean a rejection of the rule of law or the importance of law in governing society. It was not an appeal to anarchy, but to a better and more just society. The person who engages in civil disobedience shows their respect for law by accepting the consequences that might flow from an open and public breach of a law.

Rawls did not support civil disobedience as a primary option to try to persuade others in society, since that could lead to chaos. In his view, the option of civil disobedience should be confined to situations where the government has blatantly infringed the principle of equal liberty or equality of opportunity. Examples he gave included refusal of a right to vote, and laws aimed at repressing certain religious groups or denying others various opportunities.[29] A further condition was that appeals to the political majority have failed, and legal avenues have been of no avail.[30]

Those conditions are unlikely to occur in a democratic society, but they may do so. In various democracies around the Western world, the boundaries of voting constituencies have been rigged in artificial ways to ensure a majority for one party. For example, people inclined to vote for one party might be heavily concentrated within a few constituencies, leaving the majority of constituencies able to be won by the other party. This is known as 'gerrymandering'. Of course, one party's 'gerrymandering' is another's 'legitimate redrawing of constituency boundaries'.

In the United States, the Supreme Court has taken the position that if a state legislature draws boundaries for partisan political

---

27   J Rawls, *A Theory of Justice*, Oxford University Press, 1971, p 369.
28   Rawls, *A Theory of Justice*, p 364.
29   Rawls, *A Theory of Justice*, p 372.
30   Rawls, *A Theory of Justice*, p 374.

purposes, this cannot be challenged in a federal court. Specifically, it has held that a legislature may pursue partisan ends when it engages in redistricting. However, if a legislature gives race a predominant role in redistricting decisions, the resulting map may be held to be unconstitutional.[31] Race and voting preference may overlap to a very high degree. But if a state's defence to a claim of gerrymandering is to acknowledge openly that it has done so, but it says it did this for political purposes rather than on racial grounds, it will be necessary for the complainant to try to disprove that motivation.[32]

The point as relates to civil disobedience is this: voters whose political party attracts the allegiance of a majority of the voting population but who are disenfranchised by admitted partisan gerrymandering may, on Rawls' approach, have little choice but to engage in non-violent civil disobedience.

Not of this world

For Christians, public civil disobedience presents another option— one not to be entertained lightly, but one that is valid where there is a need for public protest, and where obedience to the law might demonstrate acquiescence in an unjust society. Should white South African Christians, for example, have engaged in civil disobedience to protest apartheid during much of the 20th century? It would be hard to argue that they should not have done so. Economically, they benefited greatly from the concentration of wealth and political power in their hands. Should not Christians have called their compatriots to acknowledge the moral claims of the black majority to participate fully in the society?

We must never lose sight of the fact that Jesus' kingdom is "not of this world" (John 18:36). He was not a political messiah, and we stray from our mission if we see promoting justice on earth as being the focus of all our activities as the people of God.

However, some are called to serve in this way. And that service

31 *Alexander v South Carolina NAACP* [2024].
32 See Justice Alito's majority opinion in *Alexander v South Carolina*.

might require public disobedience as a form of legitimate protest, provided that the importance of obedience to law is fully weighed in the balance, and that lawful means of persuading the government or remedying injustice through the courts have failed.

7

WHAT DOES IT MEAN TO OBEY THE LAW?

How do biblical principles about submission to government apply in the modern administrative state?

In answering such a question, it is important to recognize that the contemporary question of obedience to law arises in quite different circumstances from those of the New Testament. The modern reach of the law is very different from the idea of law that prevailed in previous centuries when the church's leading theologians grappled with the issue of whether to rise up against a tyrannical king or emperor. In Roman times, the law could be read in a single volume.[1] In contrast, the law in a modern administrative state is voluminous and has a range of different functions unknown in biblical times. In Australia, the federal Parliament passes an average of 140 new laws each year,[2] not to mention State or Territory parliaments. In addition, each year governments introduce a large volume of regulations, authorized by Parliament, to deal with matters of detail.

In the modern law, there is not a binary choice between obeying

---

1 E.g. *The Institutes of Gaius* (c 170 AD).
2 'Approximately how many bills are introduced in Parliament and passed each year?', Parliamentary Education Office (peo.gov.au/understand-our-parliament/your-questions-on-notice/questions/approximately-how-many-bills-are-introduced-in-parliament-and-passed-each-year).

and disobeying the law. It is a much more complex issue than that. The arguments cannot be confined, as they have so often been in moral philosophy, to questions about when civil disobedience is justified. The question about obedience to law needs to be answered with reference to the kind of law we are talking about and the obligations that it imposes.

Criminal law and civil law

There is an important distinction to be drawn between laws that are enforced by the State through prosecutions, and laws that give rise to some form of remedy to affected individuals if they wish to pursue it. If we are to understand the Christian's relationship to 'the law', it's important to think about the nature of criminal law and civil law in a bit of detail.

To a large extent, the criminal law is the law of "thou shalt not". It is possible to have complete obedience to the criminal law by refraining from doing what is prohibited. Most of us, whether Christians or not, do that because the criminal law conforms to our values. We are not much inclined to commit burglaries, and it is not the fear of being caught that stops us from practising our lock-picking techniques.

When Paul was writing in Romans 13 about obedience to law, he was referring to the law enforced through the punitive powers of the State. "Let everyone be subject to the governing authorities … whoever rebels against the authority is rebelling against what God has instituted … rulers do not bear the sword for no reason" (Rom 13:1–4). Other key New Testament passages are similar (Titus 3:1; 1 Pet 2:13–17). In other words, the command to obey rulers and to submit to government is in particular a command to respect the role of government in providing law and order, subject to the limitation that believers will sometimes be faced with a stark choice between obedience to government and obedience to God.

Civil disputes are quite different from the criminal law. Contract disputes are an example of this distinction. Contracts are only enforced if one of the parties wants to do so. Often, if they hit problems, they negotiate a variation to the contract or forgive breaches.

The State, through the judiciary and the courts, operates as a neutral arbiter of disputes if need be, but only if one of the parties decides to litigate the matter.

It doesn't make much sense to talk about 'obeying' the law of contract in the same way that we talk about obeying the law that prohibits murder or sexual assault. These laws are different in kind. Businesses typically abide by their contracts not because they have a moral obligation to submit to government, but because this is likely to be in the best interests of the business. No-one wants to spend time and money fighting a lawsuit through the court if that can be avoided. Many disputes are settled quietly without the matter going to court, and without reliance on the letter of the contract.

The State has no particular interest in the resolution of most civil disputes, other than that they be resolved peacefully. Any settlement of a dispute that sufficiently satisfies the parties is a good settlement from the government's point of view, whatever the legal rights-and-wrongs might be.

So, we don't 'obey' the civil law in the same way that we obey the criminal law. The civil law provides remedies to people who can prove a breach of another person's obligations towards them, if they choose to pursue those remedies. We therefore must be mindful of our obligations and of the possibility that someone will take legal action against us if they believe they have been wronged.

Dispute resolution

Resolution of civil disputes through negotiation or mediation is the norm. In fact, the vast majority of civil disputes are settled without the need for a judicial decision. Judges, in case-management hearings prior to setting a case down for trial, will usually urge the parties to settle, or will inquire of the parties whether they have made formal offers to settle. Not infrequently, judges will put a lot of subtle (or sometimes not-so-subtle!) pressure on parties to resolve their dispute by mediation or negotiation, not least to reduce the long queue of cases that might need a judicial ruling. In some areas of law, mediation may be mandatory unless the parties are exempted.[3]

The role of the law in such cases is not so much to determine how the dispute should be resolved as to establish a process by which it can be settled. There are many exit ramps off the litigation freeway; if those exit ramps are not taken, then the dispute will be resolved by a judicial decision, but that is a last resort.

In the consensual resolution of the dispute, of course the law plays some role. If the law and the facts are both on the side of one party, that will affect the other party's willingness to reach a settlement. But many civil disputes involve competing accounts of the facts. A legal remedy will only be available if certain facts are found or admitted.

Anti-discrimination claims provide an example. An applicant for a job may complain that she was not selected for the position due to discrimination on some basis such as her race, her disability, or that she does not ascribe to the faith of the employer. Her complaint of discrimination might have merit, but many factors go into the employer's decision to select candidate D from a short-listed field comprising candidates A-E (a list that may well have been drawn up from a much larger field of applicants). Of course, in selecting a person for a position, academic qualifications count for something; applicants may be required to have a degree in a particular field of study. But provided a Bachelor's degree is sufficient, a Master's degree may not make an applicant any more deserving of being hired. Factors such as the way someone presents in an interview, and how likely they are to be a good fit with the organization as a whole, are among numerous factors that may play a role in the employer's final choice.

A candidate's complaint of discrimination may therefore turn on questions of fact that would need to be resolved in their favour before any question of liability arises. Uncertainty about how the judge will view the evidence and the credibility of the witnesses may lead to a negotiated compromise settlement.

Even in civil disputes where the basic facts are not in doubt and

---

3   See, for example, *Family Law Act 1975* (Australia) s 60I. Mediation is mandatory in a parenting dispute, except where there are allegations of violence or child abuse.

liability is admitted, the real dispute may be about what level of compensation should be paid. Lawyers may put forward an unreasonable ambit claim for compensation, or the defendant may offer only a miserable sum in response. Mediation and negotiation are means of closing the gap between the two positions.

So, the civil law dictates rights and obligations that people have towards one another, and provides some parameters within which the parties can resolve disputes about those rights and obligations. The civil law may not dictate a particular outcome. Rather, a judge may impose a result if the parties cannot work it out for themselves.

Jesus' teaching on civil disputes

Jesus' advice on civil disputes is simple yet insightful: settle these matters sooner rather than later.

> "Settle matters quickly with your adversary who is taking you to court. Do it while you are still together on the way, or your adversary may hand you over to the judge, and the judge may hand you over to the officer, and you may be thrown into prison. Truly I tell you, you will not get out until you have paid the last penny." (Matt 5:25)

Jesus is saying that we are to settle disputes promptly where we owe money or are liable to pay compensation. If the matter goes to court, it will be much worse than settling early. Why? Because not only does the judge have the power to decide who owes what to whom; in those days, the judge could also imprison a person who did not pay his debts. Imprisonment provided an incentive for the debtor to find a means to pay—for example, by borrowing from a family member. Far better to resolve a dispute early and avoid the risk of being imprisoned for non-payment. In modern times, the cost of litigation is reason enough to resolve the dispute, for failure to do so can leave everyone except the lawyers far poorer.

A few years ago, I was asked to travel to another city in Australia to argue some points of law in a case that involved considerable legal complexity. The case concerned a couple who had separated, and the dispute was about the division of property, including a valuable family home. By the time of the hearing in which I was involved, the case had already been running in court for eight years. It had twice gone to an appeal court on issues of law before being sent back to a trial judge to determine the matter.

There is no doubt that at the time they separated, this couple was well off compared to most people. The husband's family had done well in business. But by the time of the hearing in which I appeared, legal costs had severely depleted their assets. My client had had to borrow to pay legal fees, and the lender was charging a high rate of interest. While in that city, I did what I could to settle the whole matter, but to no avail. Eventually, after two days of legal argument, and a very long wait for a judgement, we won that part of the case. But that meant the matter needed to go to yet another hearing. Ten years later—that is, 18 years after the case commenced and after yet more legal issues—the dispute has still not been finally resolved at the time of writing. Millions of dollars have already been spent on legal fees, almost certainly exhausting the assets of the parties, and leaving at least one of the parties with considerable debts. Had the case been settled early on and with appropriate compromises, the parties could have left their marriage with their wealth substantially intact.

The modern movement to encourage mediation is consistent with Jesus' teaching on dispute resolution. In a mediation, each party to the dispute is given an opportunity to be heard without interruption from the other. The mediator's role is to structure the subsequent discussion of the issues and to help the parties towards constructive and even creative ways of resolving them. In this process, legal rights often take second place to finding ways for those in dispute to reach an agreement. This is not to say legal rights are irrelevant, for the best alternative to a negotiated settlement may well be to press the legal claim by going to trial. However, litigation is likely to be the end of any working relationship between the parties, and each may have a greater interest in resolving the dispute peacefully than in seeking vindication through the courts.

What, then, is a Christian approach to the resolution of civil disputes? Here we should turn to the apostle Paul for his specific insight.

Paul's teaching on civil disputes

Paul taught that Christian believers should not even go off to the secular courts at all. Instead, they should look to find ways to resolve disputes within the fellowship:

> If any of you has a dispute with another, do you dare to take it before the ungodly for judgement instead of before the Lord's people? Or do you not know that the Lord's people will judge the world? And if you are to judge the world, are you not competent to judge trivial cases? Do you not know that we will judge angels? How much more the things of this life! Therefore, if you have disputes about such matters, do you ask for a ruling from those whose way of life is scorned in the church? I say this to shame you. Is it possible that there is nobody among you wise enough to judge a dispute between believers? (1 Cor 6:1–5)

Paul's reason that Christians should eschew secular courts is explicitly *theological*: Christians will share in God's work of judging the world and angels (although what that might involve, and for whom, is not spelled out). If Christians are to have such significant responsibilities, we can certainly adjudicate our own (relatively) small disputes within the people of God.

Paul then goes on to say we should rather be wronged than run off to the secular courts to enforce our rights:

> The very fact that you have lawsuits among you means you have been completely defeated already. Why not rather be wronged? Why not rather be cheated? (v 7)

This is consistent with Jesus' teaching in the Sermon on the Mount (Matt 5:40).

Paul's teaching here is specifically about disputes between Christians. In most other cases where we find ourselves in a legal dispute that might involve court action, a Christian approach will involve seeking peace with the person who is on the other side of the dispute, engaging in mediation or other good faith negotiation. This may not be true of all cases. Some civil claims may be brought with an ulterior motive, such as advancing a cause, harassing people with whose views the person disagrees, or seeking unwarranted compensation. Some claims for compensation—for example, from harm that is alleged to have occurred a long time ago, or in circumstances where there are no living witnesses—could be mistaken or even fraudulent. Not all civil complaints are made in good faith because of a genuine grievance. A decision to settle such claims might be made on a commercial basis to save time and legal fees, but this can invite further claims of the same kind, just as paying ransom money may lead to more kidnapping.

Regulation in the modern administrative state

In seeking to understand what it means for a Christian to comply with the law, the distinction between the criminal and civil law is important. A particular kind of civil law is government regulation. Companies, for example, are subject to a vast array of legal requirements, as are various industries. These laws are not enforced by the police and are not prosecuted in the criminal courts. If they need to be enforced, this occurs by means of fines imposed by the same courts that hear civil disputes. Other penalties might include, for example, disqualification from holding office as a director.

Many parliaments around the world pass thousands upon thousands of pages of new or revised laws and regulations every year. Much of the detailed regulation comes from government departments imposing requirements based upon broad parliamentary authority. Typically, the laws that governments pass are not matched by the allocation of sufficient new resources to enforce them effectively. Wherever possible, government agencies encourage voluntary compliance and have little capacity to do otherwise. Regulatory agencies and courts are already over-stretched. Inevitably, therefore, enforcement is highly selective and typically confined to egregious breaches of regulations. Regulatory law is different in kind both from the criminal law and the law concerning the resolution of private disputes.

Whatever we may think about specific regulations or the cumulative burden of 'red tape', regulatory law should be seen as part of the work of government to which we are called to submit. As Christians, we ought to have great respect for law, strive to obey it where we know its requirements, and understand that governments—even those with which we disagree on many matters—are ordained by God.

That said, law is a blunt instrument of regulation. The same requirements often apply to three-person companies or small not-for-profit organizations as to multinational businesses. For a small organization, it may not be realistic to try to comply fully with all the requirements. Even knowing what they are can be a considerable task. Organizations subject to such regulations often need to make sensible decisions about how fulsome their compliance with the law's various demands should be in the circumstances of their particular business or organization. Such decisions are made, knowing that on many issues a regulatory agency will have no interest in taking enforcement action.

A failure to obey a regulatory law may not involve any moral fault at all. For example, if a law requires me to renew a licence by a certain date, I should do so. If I forget and am a week late, I might be required to pay a late fee. But my failure to comply with this law is of a different character to breaking the kinds of law Paul was concerned with in Romans 13 and similar passages. I submit to government either by renewing my licence on time or paying the late fee if it is imposed. Either way, I am submitting to the authority of government and respecting the law. Christians who violate these kinds of laws—especially if they do so inadvertently—need not carry around a guilty conscience.

The concentric circles of compliance

There are various kinds of regulatory laws. Some require positive actions, such as applying for planning permission before conducting major building works or providing information on an annual basis to the regulator of a corporation. There are only three responses to positive obligations: comply; comply late (where there is a due date); or fail to comply.

Other requirements are expressed in general terms and do not dictate any particular course of action. Workers' health-and-safety legislation is an example of this. The core obligation is to maintain a safe workplace, but how much effort will be put into workplace health-and-safety compliance will depend on the nature of the organization or business.

In such circumstances, compliance with the law is likely to involve concentric circles. The small inner circles represent the core things that the organization must do, such as responding promptly where an employee identifies a clear hazard that needs to be reduced or eliminated. At the next level out, there are things that ought to be done on a regular basis (e.g. checking that fire equipment works and that a first-aid kit is adequately stocked). Then there are things that would be good to do (e.g. have fire wardens to help manage evacuations), and many other things that could be done, depending upon the risk of injury or other harm in that workplace.

When someone asserts that such-and-such is required by workplace health-and-safety law, and their demand for compliance appears unreasonable, it is worth exploring what they understand the legal requirement to be. The most extreme version of 'what the law requires'—in health and safety, or in many others areas—takes the organization to the outer perimeter of the law's concentric circles of compliance.

Just as compliance with health-and-safety laws will depend on the activity conducted and the risk of injury in that workplace, so legal risk arising from non-compliance needs to be understood in a similar way. Some legal risks are remote because, while it is possible to interpret the law as applying in given circumstances, the risk of harm is low, and regulators are unlikely to take enforcement action. How much should someone's interpretation of how the law might apply affect the organization's decisions?

In other words, is the cost of compliance worth it?

Case study: A debate about an issue of church governance

An example of this question arose in the Presbyterian Church of NSW, which forbade discussion of certain topics in its General Assembly because to do so would, it was advised, risk breaching workplace health-and-safety laws.[4] The presenting issue was the Assembly's decision to consider legislation that would permit only male elders. A paper on the issue was circulated. At the present time, there is no such restriction on who can be an elder in the Presbyterian Church of NSW. Changing the rules was no doubt a very controversial proposition.

Shortly before its assembly in 2023, the Church leadership received a letter from a member of the Church concerning the dissemination of the paper, and complaining about the lack of 'psychosocial trauma support' provided during discussion of its contents. Legal advice received just before the Assembly said there was a risk of contravening the workplace health-and-safety law.[5] The Assembly resolved to delay consideration of the matter until the Trustees had received fuller legal advice.

After the Assembly, the Trustees sought legal advice from a senior lawyer through the Church's legal officers. This advice confirmed that the workplace health-and-safety law applied to the Assembly's deliberations, although the contents of that advice were not shared with members. The argument that discussion in a church assembly could be in breach of NSW workplace health and safety law likely arises from the law's requirement to consult with 'workers' on matters that could affect safety. The argument would be along the lines that 'workers' includes volunteers. Elders are volunteers. The argument might be that a change to the Church's rules could cause psychological harm to volunteers and so is an issue of workplace safety. Those who aspire to eldership in the future also

---

4   For two accounts of this, see J Sandeman, 'When can the government tell churches what to do', *TheOtherCheek.com*, 31 July 2024 (theothercheek.com.au/when-can-the-government-tell-churches-what-to-do) and D Robertson, 'Erastianism in the church', *AP*, 25 July 2024 (ap.org.au/2024/07/25/erastianism-in-the-church).
5   *Work Health and Safety Act 2011* (NSW).

needed to be consulted as they might suffer psychological harm. Therefore, debate on the issue could not proceed without consulting everyone who might be affected. The specific risk of not so doing was that workplace safety regulators could have prosecuted the Church for breach of the law.

The Trustees reported that, based on this advice, the Assembly should develop a "responsive and inclusive approach" to consider the matter. At the 2024 Assembly, a motion was passed "that the sex qualifications of elders shall not be the subject of questions, speeches, comments or debate for the duration of this session of Assembly".[6] A committee was established to set up a consultation process that would comply with workplace health-and-safety law with a view to bringing recommendations back to the next Assembly.

There are plenty of good reasons why consultation with elders of local churches and other interested members is highly desirable, particularly when a change might be controversial and risk the denomination losing members. On the other hand, such a view on the application of workplace health-and-safety law would make any church governance unworkable. If the spectre of 'psychological harm' could be so readily invoked to shut down discussion, and if legal questions arise as to whether Parliament intended the workplace health-and-safety law to take such a wide view of 'harm', it would become difficult for organizations to function. The same arguments could be applied to countless other issues where there is a potential clash between theological positions and prevailing cultural understandings of 'equality' and 'non-discrimination'.

In dealing with threats of this kind from a biblical perspective, several questions need to be asked. First, what was the intention of Parliament in enacting the law? Second, is it likely that Parliament intended the view of the law that has been advanced? Third, what is the likelihood of legal action being taken if the organization does not comply with the understanding of the law that is being urged upon it? Fourth, is it likely that such legal action would succeed? Fifth, what are the likely consequences if legal action does succeed?

6   D Robertson, 'Erastianism in the church'.

Sixth, would adhering to the view of the law that has been advanced interfere significantly with the core business of the organization? Seventh, if there is some kind of legal risk, what is the organization's risk appetite?

The last of these questions would be asked by any business faced with an unreasonable demand based upon a particular view of how a broad and general law applies in a given context. Legal advice on such matters is not always helpful, for lawyers will often give the most conservative answer to any legal question. That is, if someone asks whether a course of action involves a legal risk, and there is some doubt about how wide the concentric circles of the law go, the safe legal answer is to assume the law's maximum reach and to advise against the proposed course of action. But this is not always helpful, especially if it imposes unnecessary constraints or burdens on the organization. There has to be an assessment of the magnitude of the risk.

When it comes to predicting the decisions of regulators, it is worth remembering that the best way to undermine respect for a law is to insist on an unreasonable application of it. Regulators with limited resources will be well aware of that, and are therefore unlikely to pursue enforcement applications at the periphery of the law's concerns. They are much more likely to concentrate on egregious breches of the law.

Activist interpretations of the law

In thinking about compliance, another hazard is how to respond to official interpretations of the law that seem to exceed what the law requires. Sometimes organizations will—either deliberately, or from an excess of enthusiasm for their cause—say that the law requires this or that when it does nothing of the sort. In other words, it might be necessary to look behind claims about the law and to form an independent judgement—including getting legal advice, should the circumstances require it.

If someone says that the law requires x or y, and that sounds incredible or too bad to be true, there is at least some likelihood it is not true. An illustration of this is the interpretation of a 'conversion therapy' law that was given by the responsible regulatory agency in the Australian state of Victoria. The *Change or Suppression (Conversion) Practices Prohibition Act 2021* makes it an offence to engage in a "change or suppression practice" in relation to a person's sexual orientation or gender identity. This is defined as a practice or conduct directed towards a person for the purpose of "changing or suppressing the sexual orientation or gender identity of the person; or inducing the person to change or suppress their sexual orientation or gender identity".[7]

This legislation gives enforcement powers to the Victorian Human Rights and Equal Opportunity Commission, which, for a long time, gave this as an example of a 'conversion practice':

> A parent refusing to support their child's request for medical treatment that will enable them to prevent physical changes from puberty that do not align with the child's gender identity and denying their child access to any health care services that would affirm their child's gender identity.[8]

In other words, the advice given was that the parent *must* take the child to a medical practitioner who is prepared to prescribe puberty blockers to prevent the onset or continuation of the child's normal pubertal development.

This illustration was clearly wrong in law. Under the legislation, prohibited conduct must involve a practice or conduct which is active in nature. It must either aim to change or suppress a person's sexual orientation or gender identity, or to induce a person to do so. One cannot engage in a 'change or suppression practice' by omission. Furthermore, simply refusing to take a child to a doctor for medical intervention does nothing to change the child's 'gender identity'. The Commission was made aware that its position was not

---

7   *Change or Suppression (Conversion) Practices Act 2021* (Victoria), section 5(1) (legislation.vic.gov.au/as-made/acts/change-or-suppression-conversion-practices-prohibition-act-2021).

8   See K Smith, 'Victorians can't ask for help under these laws', *Binary Australia*, 18 August 2022 (binary.org.au/victorians_can_t_ask_for_help_under_these_laws).

legally tenable, and backed off its extreme position.[9] But it wasn't until two years later that it chose to remove the example from its website—and only after international controversies about the safety and suitability of puberty blockers as a response to childhood gender incongruence.[10]

When activists who are passionate for a cause work for a regulatory organization, overreach is an ever-present risk. Their interpretations of the law cannot be taken necessarily as representing a fair reading of it. Threats of legal action based upon such overreach may be empty.

When limited compliance may be appropriate

How, then, should Christians respond when government overreaches its legitimate role in ensuring the peace, order and good governance of the society? How should we respond when the government seeks to impose unreasonable obligations or restraints on churches?

As a possible example, consider another law passed in Victoria: the *Child Wellbeing and Safety (Child Safe Standards Compliance and Enforcement) Amendment Act 2021*. This law requires organizations that work with children to observe various requirements relating to child safety. To a large extent, these are based upon the National Principles for Child Safe Organizations that were developed following a five-year-long Royal Commission into child sexual abuse in churches, schools, children's homes, and other institutions.[11] The principles developed by the Royal Commission were intended to be applied flexibly, taking account of the nature and purpose of the organization. They were also concerned only with child sexual abuse.

9   B Lane, '"Overreach" by conversion therapy watchdog', *Gender Clinic News*, 1 June 2022 (www.genderclinicnews.com/p/overreach-by-conversion-therapy-watchdog).

10   B Lane, 'Memory holes and insider rules', *Gender Clinic News*, 20 March 2024 (www. genderclinicnews.com/p/memory-holes-and-insider-rules).

11   See 'National Principles for Child Safe Organizations' on the Australian Government website (childsafety.gov.au/resources/national-principles-child-safe-organisations); see also the website for the Royal Commission into Institutional Responses to Child Sexual Abuse at childabuseroyalcommission.gov.au.

However, Victoria chose to turn these flexible and important principles into mandatory minimum requirements, backed up with enforcement provisions, including fines. These minimum requirements apply to a vast array of organizations, large and small, volunteer-run or professional.[12] These include small voluntary organizations, such as a local club which organizes sports team for children or a drama society which involves children under 18 in its productions. They also apply to small organizations established for a limited purpose, such as a piano school. All religious organizations are included.

While many of these standards are appropriate, and indeed necessary to reduce the risk of child abuse by staff or volunteers, others are only tangentially related to child protection. The list of obligations is very long and, in places, quite aspirational, notwithstanding that these are said to be *minimum* requirements.[13] Thus all organizations are under a duty to ensure racism within the organization is identified, confronted, and not tolerated. That may be a good thing, but it is somewhat remote from core child-safety concerns.

Standard 3 of the Act provides another illustration of the obligations now placed on every organization. This Standard provides that:

Children and young people are empowered about their rights, participate in decisions affecting them and are taken seriously.

In complying with Child Safe Standard 3 an organization must, at a minimum, ensure:

- Children and young people are informed about all of their rights, including to safety, information and participation.
- The importance of friendships is recognised and support from peers is encouraged, to help children and young people feel safe and be less isolated.
- Organizations have strategies in place to develop a culture that facilitates participation and is responsive to the input of children and young people.

12 *Child Wellbeing and Safety Act 2005*, s 9 and schedule 1.
13 See 'The 11 Child Safe Standards' on the Commission for Children and Young People website (ccyp.vic.gov.au/child-safe-standards/the-11-child-safe-standards).

- Organizations provide opportunities for children and young people to participate and are responsive to their contributions, thereby strengthening confidence and engagement.[14]

Accompanying these minimum requirements are various expectations about documents. These include age-appropriate and easy-to-understand documents, which must be easily accessible (in print and online), and which must support children to understand their rights—including their rights to safety, information, and participation. These requirements make sense for a school that has children on site for several hours per day for most of the year. They make rather less sense for a mothers and toddlers play group in a local church, given that children at this age can't read.

Another example of overreach is in the training requirements. Not only must staff and volunteers be trained in identifying indicators of child abuse and harm; they must also receive training and information on "how to build culturally safe environments for children and young people". This is not confined to issues concerning respecting the culture of Indigenous children and young people. Without that context, 'cultural safety' is an exceedingly vague term.

None of the requirements in the Victorian standards represent undesirable goals, of course. Indeed, they may well be very desirable goals. However, imposing the same positive and resource-intensive obligations on a mothers and toddlers group or a small piano school as on the Department of Education schools represents a clear case of overreach. If taken seriously, the burden of compliance on small organizations, particularly those run by volunteers, is considerable.

In practice, such laws are largely unenforceable. They rely almost entirely on voluntary compliance by organizations that are not licensed, accredited or otherwise actively supervised by a government body. The relevant government agency would not even be able to compile a list of all the organizations that it purports to regulate.

---

14 Commission for Children and Young People, 'Standard 3: Children and young people are empowered about their rights, participate in decisions affecting them and are taken seriously' (ccyp.vic.gov.au/child-safe-standards/the-11-child-safe-standards/standard-3).

How should a church or other Christian ministry respond to laws of this kind? Here, it may be useful again to think of concentric circles. There are core obligations, such as having a child-protection policy and training for volunteers working with children. Standard 2 of the Victorian law cited above is that "child safety and wellbeing is embedded in organizational leadership, governance and culture". This is also highly desirable. The standards require care in the selection of volunteers to work with children, including appropriate screening. All of these fall within the inner circle of obligations to try to ensure the safety and wellbeing of children and young people who take part in the activities of the church.

But other aspects of the law may not fit so neatly. For example, Standard 3 (cited above) requires organizations to ensure that "the importance of friendships is recognised and support from peers is encouraged". How does a church comply with this type of requirement, when "friendship" may fall outside the primary scope of its ministry? If a church runs a Sunday school, its work is confined to providing Sunday morning classes for children during the church gathering, with the aim of teaching children something about the Christian faith. Helping children to form friendships may be a happy byproduct of these activities, but it is not the core purpose of the activity.

In determining how far the church should seek to comply with obligations that may not be well-thought through and fit for purpose in its context, it may be worth asking: what is a proportionate response to the obligation, given the scope of our work and the resources available to us? A proportionate response should involve full compliance with the core child-protection obligations. There should also be at least a reasonable attempt to comply with obligations in the outer circles where children's safety is not at stake. Churches and ministries might consider it appropriate to engage in no more than token compliance with other obligations that are disproportionate, given their activities and purposes. For example, if the government wants every child in every organization to know about all of their rights, children could be given a link to the UN

Convention on the Rights of the Child,[15] or the church could give it to their parents. Is this sufficient compliance? What is sufficient is a matter of opinion and degree, given the context of the organization's work.[16]

Denominations can, of course, assist local churches in meeting their obligations. In fact, this can be one of a denomination's most important functions. For example, in the case of the Victorian law on child safety, the denomination might write a generic policy statement to which all local churches adhere. This statement could commit the churches in general terms to the values that the Standards seek to promote. Volunteers working with children could be asked to read that policy. If the government wants training in cultural safety, volunteers might be given a link to a website that explains the concept.[17] In practical terms, the obligations would have to be read in the context of the age group of the children involved in the church, and of how much time those children spend in its activities.

None of this is to suggest that Christian groups and organizations should do other than take the obligation of compliance seriously. We are to be good citizens, both individually and corporately. A badly run ministry that makes little effort to comply with applicable laws is at the very least a bad witness. Worse, it may be exposed to consequences, such as fines, that could have been avoided with better management and care.

However, sometimes there are reasons why compliance might be less than complete. Large organizations such as banks have substantial resources devoted to compliance. It is typically not possible for small organizations, particularly those run by volunteers, to devote

15 United Nations Human Rights, 'Convention on the Rights of the Child', *United Nations*, 1989 (www.ohchr.org/en/instruments-mechanisms/instruments/convention-rights-child).

16 It is hard to imagine that parents send their children to Sunday school with the expectation that the children will learn what the United Nations thinks about their rights. It may arouse opposition. However, this is the risk that governments take in overreaching their legitimate role. The law falls into disrepute, and the political party introducing such requirements may suffer electoral backlash.

17 Australian Human Rights Commission, 'Cultural safety', *Child Safe Organizations* (childsafe.humanrights.gov.au/diverse-needs/cultural-safety).

the same resources. Government regulatory agencies are mindful of this in determining how to respond to a possible breach (e.g. with a reminder letter, or by imposing a penalty).

Above all, churches should keep the main thing the main thing: in obedience to the word of God, boldly proclaim Christ to one another and to our communities. Our obedience to the laws of the land is important, but we should not take upon ourselves and our ministries an unnecessary burden—either as a consequence of over-zealous compliance with unreasonable laws, or by giving the broadest possible interpretation to what the law might require.

PART III

WHEN LAW COMES INTO
CONFLICT WITH MINISTRY

8

LIVING PEACEABLE LIVES

How do we avoid unnecessary legal trouble?

Paul wrote in his first letter to Timothy:

> I urge, then, first of all, that petitions, prayers, intercession and thanksgiving be made for all people—for kings and all those in authority, that we may live peaceful and quiet lives in all godliness and holiness. This is good, and pleases God our Saviour, who wants all people to be saved and to come to a knowledge of the truth. (1 Tim 2:1–3)

As Christians and as churches, our primary concern in relation to government ought to be that the system of law and government provides a framework in which we can live peaceful and quiet lives and be able to share the gospel. For centuries, Christians in the Western world have been able to live in such a society.

The reality now is that in many parts of the Western world, we are not in the same benign situation. There is growing hostility to faith, or contempt for faith. Religious freedom is, to some extent, being restricted. Law is also being weaponized in various ways by people bringing complaints aimed at achieving change, rather than merely seeking compensation for a perceived wrong.

How do we respond to such challenges? There are a number of principles.

Pick your battles

As Christians, we are called to high standards in terms of how we treat others, including those who disagree with us or whose beliefs we do not share. Paul wrote to Timothy, giving this advice:

> Don't have anything to do with foolish and stupid arguments, because you know they produce quarrels. And the Lord's servant must not be quarrelsome but must be kind to everyone …
> (2 Tim 2:23–24)

In the family of God, we all have different callings. Some will be called to a public life in politics or the media. That may involve talking about contentious issues in the public square. That is not the calling of the great majority of us, but for those for whom it is part of their ministry, there can be a heightened legal risk: those who argue in the public square on contentious 'culture war' issues are the most likely to become the targets of attack.

There was once a time when such debates occurred almost entirely through the presentation of competing ideas. Through such publicly accessible debates, people could be assisted to work out their own position. Increasingly, however, the war of ideas is supported by 'lawfare'—the invocation of proceedings in courts and tribunals that have, and are no doubt designed to have, a chilling effect on the expression of certain kinds of religious belief. In particular, laws prohibiting discrimination and vilification can be weaponized, as we saw in chapter 3. These can be used to try to silence a viewpoint with which complainants disagree.

There are battles to be fought in the public square on various social issues. However, those of us called to do so need to pick our battles carefully and to engage in such debates with wisdom and grace. Fighting every battle with similar intensity and effort may seem heroic, but it is not how generals win wars. They choose where, when and how to fight, with a view to winning the war as a whole. Winning may involve losing some battles, avoiding others, or engaging in strategic retreats.

Consider, for example, whether we should be involved in action against drag queens reading stories to little children in public libraries. Many libraries across the Western world have chosen to host such an event for small children as part of their events program. Such events have been promoted as part of an orchestrated activist campaign that has a social (and perhaps political) purpose. A leading organization for such events is Drag Story Hour (DSH), founded in San Francisco in 2015.[1] In the 'about us' section of its website, the organizers say this:

> It's just what it sounds like! Storytellers using the art of drag to read books to kids in libraries, schools, and bookstores. DSH captures the imagination and play of the gender fluidity of childhood and gives kids glamorous, positive, and unabashedly queer role models.

While drag queens are strongly associated with the LGBTQ+ movement, their work with little children does not itself create much of a role model for being transgender. The kind of exaggerated and extravagant dress and make-up of drag queens has little to do with how women dress or act in their day-to-day lives. Gender dysphoric males who seek to 'pass' as females do not, typically, draw attention to themselves; the great majority want to be accepted as they are, and to get on with their lives quietly. So, it is a little unclear what the DSH movement is trying to achieve other than to celebrate cross-dressing.

However, at the very least, the intention is to promote the idea that it is glamorous and positive to be 'queer'. The term 'queer' doesn't really have a stable and well-defined meaning. It used to be synonymous with being gay or lesbian, but it is no longer so limited. It now embraces people who hold a great variety of different beliefs and understandings about gender or about their own sexuality.

In January 2020, Wilson Gavin, a devout Catholic man and President of the conservative political association at his university, took part in a protest against a Drag Queen Story Time event at the Brisbane State Library. The event was organized by Rainbow Families

---

1   This used to be called 'Drag Queen Story Hour'. Now they include 'kings'. See dragstoryhour.org.

Queensland. Mr Gavin also publicly identified as gay. The protesters sought to disrupt the event, chanting "drag queens are not for kids". That was no doubt a frightening experience for some of the young children present. There was a strong social-media backlash against the protest after videos of it circulated online. The next day, tragically, Mr Gavin committed suicide.[2]

Not long afterwards, a well-known Christian commentator published a blog post in which he made adverse comments about the two performers that day. One of them was born female but has adopted a male identification; the other is a gay male. That article led to hugely expensive litigation against the Christian commentator. Such cases tend to be brought by well-funded and government-supported LGBTQ+ legal organizations, and are not easily settled. The complaint was that the article had vilified the two performers based upon their sexual orientation or gender identity. The claim was rejected by the tribunal, but only after more than $300,000 was spent in defending the case.[3] At time of writing, it has gone on appeal, which will mean considerable further expense.

In retrospect, was this particular battle against the Drag Queen Story Time worth it? Certainly, it was not worth the tragic loss of life that occurred.

The reasons for protesting events like this are, typically, twofold: first, that such performances are unsuitable for small children; and secondly, that these events should not be hosted in publicly funded venues such as libraries.

In thinking about an issue of this kind, there are several considerations. First, the 'male pretending to be a female' trope is well-known in the entertainment industry. Examples include Barry Humphries as Dame Edna, and Robin Williams as Mrs Doubtfire. In previous generations, and no doubt still today, young children are taken to

---

2   J Sandeman, 'Wilson Gavin, a victim of the culture war', *Eternity News*, 14 January 2020 (eternitynews.com.au/australia/wilson-gavin-a-victim-of-the-culture-war); J Taylor, 'Grief over death of Young Liberal Wilson Gavin after drag queen protest', *The Guardian*, 13 January 2020 (theguardian.com/australia-news/2020/jan/14/grief-over-death-of-young-liberal-wilson-gavin-after-drag-queen-protest).
3   This figure is taken from a blog post by the person concerned.

pantomimes. They may well see two men playing the Ugly Sisters in a production of *Cinderella*. Seeing a male 'drag queen' dressing up as a woman in a highly exaggerated and flamboyant kind of way may not look very different to a small child than seeing men playing the Ugly Sisters or a similar role.

Second, even if the drag queens were reading stories that might confuse young children about what it means to be a boy or a girl, the parents brought the children to the event voluntarily. It was not being imposed upon conscript classes at school. Given that, in this case, the event was organized by a group called Rainbow Families, it is quite probable that most parents attending were already onside with the values and beliefs of this group, and the remainder were sympathetic to it.

Third, these movements tend to peter out. Drag queens seem to be 'all the rage' in LGBTQ+ activist communities at present. *RuPaul's Drag Race* has been a popular reality TV series for well over a decade. After a while, people look for something new and different. The old becomes old. Another common pattern is that transgressive or 'progressive' ideas are co-opted by large corporations to sell products. They become part of the new corporate establishment and thereby lose their anti-establishment appeal. The likely scenario for the drag-queen story-hour movement is that it will gradually fade away.

Of course, Christians ought to be concerned about these issues. The godly response to seeing biblical values eroded from our culture, or to seeing adults leading children into confusion on such important matters, will not be one of indifference. But it is important to be wise and prayerful in how to object. Sometimes it is better not to give such movements notoriety by vocal opposition.

However, once litigation was commenced against the Christian commentator, it was probably the right course to defend the case. There is a need to seek reasonable interpretations of any law that inhibits free speech on matters of public interest, and to define more clearly the boundaries of acceptable public commentary.

Don't provoke the bull

For most Christians, the best way of avoiding legal trouble is to aim to be exemplary citizens, complying with relevant laws, and not engaging in open conflict with the government or regulators where there is potential for a collision of values. There may be a bull around somewhere that could attack you if it is angered—but there is no need to wave a red rag under its nose.

Citipointe Christian College in Brisbane provides an example in which a school, seeking to be transparent about its beliefs, inadvertently provoked a bull.

In January 2022, at a time when there was a significant national debate about the rights of faith-based schools to maintain their identity and ethos, Citipointe issued a new enrolment contract to parents. This occurred just before term was to begin for a new academic year. The school insisted that parents sign it as a condition of their children remaining enrolled at the school.

The changes to the existing contract that provoked particular anger concerned gender identity and sexual orientation. The contract provided that "the college will only enrol the student on the basis of the gender that corresponds to their biological sex". This was intended to maintain consistency with the college's "Christian Ethos Requirements". It went on to state that the college "acknowledges the biological sex of a person as recognized at birth and requires practices consistent with that sex". Parents were also asked to agree to a set of religious beliefs attached to the contract. These included a statement that "any form of sexual immorality (including but not limited to; adultery, fornication, homosexual acts, bisexual acts, bestiality, incest, paedophilia, and pornography) is sinful and offensive to God and is destructive to human relationships and society".[4]

The document was intended only to make clear the beliefs and values that the school had long held. However, it resulted in uproar.

---

4   A Courty and J Randall, 'Brisbane's Citipointe Christian College defends demanding parents sign contract on student gender identity, homosexuality', *ABC News*, 31 January 2022 (abc.net.au/news/2022-01-31/qld-school-contract-lgbtqi-citipointe-christian-college/100791734).

The Minister for Education quickly referred the school to the Non-State Schools Accreditation Board, raising questions about whether the school was in breach of its legal obligations.[5]

The point is not to question whether a Christian school is right to treat children "on the basis of the gender that corresponds to their biological sex". Of course they are right to do so, just as they are right to insist that "any form of sexual immorality … is sinful and offensive to God". The point is to ask whether the issue should have been handled differently, rather than by waving the red rag in front of the bull. And the 'red rag' in this situation was to insist, without notice, and on the eve of a new academic year, that the children of any parents who declined to sign the new enrolment contract would be treated as withdrawn from the school. The amended contract stated:

> Where a parent or guardian is unwilling to provide consent and hence no longer desires to have their child or children remain in the College under this revised contract, the College will accept the withdrawal of their child or children.

If children were not allowed to continue at the school, this would disrupt their education and their friendships with peers. When changes of this kind are introduced, they at least need to be 'grandfathered'. That is, the existing enrolment contract should continue for all children currently enrolled in the school, while parents seeking to enrol their child for the first time could be asked to sign the new one.

A group of parents wrote publicly that, while they were aware the school was working on a new enrolment contract, they expected to be consulted about it:

> We imagined there would be information evenings where the proposed changes would be discussed with parents and teachers. The school could then tell us why the changes were necessary and give us an opportunity to respond. After all, contracts aren't altered unilaterally. A contract has two parties,

5   A Courty, 'Review of Brisbane's Citipointe Christian College ordered over "distressing" enrolment contract as lawyer questions its legal basis', *ABC News*, 1 February 2022 (abc.net.au/news/2022-02-01/qld-christian-citipointe-school-contract-controversy-reaction/100795490).

and each party needs to agree if the contract is amended. That's what we thought.[6]

That was not an unreasonable expectation. A few days later, after widespread condemnation of the school's position, the new enrolment contract was withdrawn.[7] Parents took the school to the Queensland Human Rights Commission. As a consequence, some two years later, it reached a settlement with them, issuing a public statement of regret.[8]

Issues of sexuality and gender are undoubtedly difficult for faith-based schools that adhere to beliefs that conflict with many of their students and parents. A great many Christian schools in Australia have a substantial proportion of children and families who are not active Christian believers. During adolescence, young people are still developing their identities, and that can involve some fluidity in terms of sexual attraction.[9] Gender identity, in particular, can give rise to complex pastoral issues, particularly when children have other mental-health problems and are seeking to go down a medical pathway, using puberty blockers and cross-sex hormones. Other students in the school may be affected—for example, where

---

6   Concerned parents of Citipointe, 'As parents of children at Citipointe Christian College, we are refusing to sign its enrolment contract—here's why', *ABC Religion and Ethics*, 1 February 2022 (abc.net.au/religion/why-we-refuse-to-sign-citipointe-college-disciminatory-contract/13736394).

7   J Randall and L Rangiah, 'Brisbane's Citipointe Christian College withdraws sexuality contract after backlash', *ABC News*, 3 February 2022 (abc.net.au/news/2022-02-03/qld-former-citipointe-christian-college-contract-withdrawn/100800748).

8   ABC News, 'Citipointe Christian College issues statement of regret two years after controversial student contract', *ABC News*, 9 June 2024 (abc.net.au/news/2024-06-09/qld-citipointe-expression-of-regret-over-lgbtiq-students/103956944).

9   The National Longitudinal Study of Adolescent Health in the USA illustrates this. Wave 1 of the study was conducted in the mid-1990s. Over 12,000 young people from Years 7–12 answered questions about romantic attractions and relationships. This cohort of young people was followed up into adulthood for many years. Over 80 per cent of boys who indicated they had a same-sex attraction at Wave 1 described themselves as exclusively heterosexual in Wave 4, 13–15 years later. Of Wave-1 girls who indicated they had any same-sex romantic attraction, 60 per cent identified as exclusively heterosexual at Wave 4 and 30 per cent were mostly heterosexual. (R Savin-Williams and K Joyner, 'The dubious assessment of gay, lesbian, and bisexual adolescents of Add Health', *Archives of Sexual Behavior*, 2014, 43(3):413–422.)

one child's gender identification has implications for other students' right to bodily privacy or fair competition in school sports. Schools need to have policies on how to deal with these matters.

The issues require sensitivity and nuance. The great majority of Christian schools no doubt navigate them well and demonstrate exemplary pastoral care to all students. Part of the sensitivity and nuance required is in how Christian teaching on sexuality or gender is presented to students and their parents, knowing that some students will experience same-sex attraction or gender incongruence.

Many churches and other Christian ministries face the same type of issues. The truth is never up for debate; God's word remains non-negotiable. But it's not only a matter of believing what is right; it's also a matter of communicating our beliefs with wisdom, gentleness and respect. Very often, that respectful approach will avoid or reduce legal trouble.

Navigate anti-discrimination laws wisely

In some jurisdictions, anti-discrimination laws provide new challenges for Christian organizations, in some cases making it very difficult for them to maintain their religious identity and ethos.

There ought to be nothing unreasonable about Christian organizations, such as schools, seeking to appoint Christians to their staff, or at least to prefer those who share the faith and mission of the organization. Article 6 of the UN Declaration on the Elimination of all Forms of Intolerance and of Discrimination Based on Religion (1981) specifically provides for the right of religions to establish and maintain appropriate charitable or humanitarian institutions. It makes no sense of such a right if the State interferes with the staffing policies of the organization by insisting that it employ people who are not Christians and whose values may be incompatible with those held by the organization. Political parties are entitled to insist that their representatives adhere to party policy.[10] Religious

10   M Chambers, 'One rule for Labor, another for religious schools', *The Catholic Weekly*, 30 July 2024 (catholicweekly.com.au/religious-schools-anti-discrimination-law-labor-government).

organizations should not be in a different position.

Increasingly, however, faith-based organizations are subject to anti-discrimination laws that limit their religious freedom in terms of staffing policy. An illustration of this is the *Equal Opportunity (Religious Exceptions) Amendment Act 2021* in Victoria. This abolished most exemptions that had previously protected the right of faith-based organizations to maintain their identity and ethos. The law deprived religious bodies of the right to select, or prefer to select, staff who adhere to the religious beliefs of the organization or to take disciplinary action against a staff member who infringes the moral values of the organization, with limited exceptions. These exceptions include:

> (a) the ordination or appointment of priests, ministers of religion or members of a religious order; or
>
> (b) the training or education of people seeking [such ordination or appointment]; or
>
> (c) the selection or appointment of people to perform functions in relation to, or otherwise participate in, any religious observance or practice.[11]

Unless those exceptions apply, religious bodies will only be able to discriminate in employment based on someone's religious belief (or lack thereof) *if* a court accepts that conformity with the doctrines, beliefs or principles of the religion is an inherent requirement of the position. Even then, the discrimination will only be lawful if, because of their beliefs, the person concerned cannot meet the inherent requirement, and if the discrimination is reasonable and proportionate in the circumstances.[12]

The test of an 'inherent requirement' is quite strict: in effect, it means that someone could not do the job without having the relevant attribute. There would be little problem in an Anglican school advertising for a chaplain who adheres to the faith of the school; but human-rights advocates are likely to take a different view about

11 *Equal Opportunity Act 2010* (Vic), s 82.
12 *Equal Opportunity Act 2010*, s 82–83A.

whether a science teacher needs to be a Christian believer.[13]

Laws of this kind are being enacted elsewhere in Australia. In 2024, the Australian Law Reform Commission made similar recommendations concerning employment in faith-based schools, albeit with a less strict test (see chapter 4).

How, then, should Christian organizations respond to such legislation when they are committed to maintaining their religious identity and ethos? It is important to have a clear understanding of what the law does and does not provide. The law in Victoria, for example, still makes it possible to discriminate on the basis of religious belief where being a Christian is an inherent requirement of the position, and where the discrimination is both "reasonable and proportionate". That is a narrow ledge, but it is at least a ledge.

Anti-discrimination law typically provides a remedy to existing employees and to applicants for employment who believe they have been subject to discrimination. As noted in chapter 7, various issues of fact might need to be determined before a case of discrimination is made out. Even when it has been shown that there was some discrimination involved, the court or tribunal will need to consider the defences available to the organization, such as whether being a Christian was legitimately an inherent requirement. The great majority of anti-discrimination complaints are resolved through confidential mediation without anyone making findings on these matters.

One way to navigate a tricky legal environment is to make the Christian ethos of the school crystal clear in all information provided to job applicants. This needs to be done in a way that does not breach the law by advertising an intention to discriminate unlawfully.[14]

---

13   See, for example, Queensland Human Rights Commission, 'Building Belonging: Review of Queensland's' Anti-Discrimination Act 1991', July 2022, recommendation 39.4 (qhrc. qld.gov.au/__data/assets/pdf_file/0012/40224/QHRC-Building-Belonging.WCAG. pdf): "The [Anti-discrimination] Act should include examples to demonstrate that the exception does not permit discrimination against employees who are not involved in the teaching, observance or practice of a religion, such as a science teacher in a religious educational institution."

14   See, for example, Queensland's Anti-Discrimination Act 1991, s 127(1): "A person must not publish or display an advertisement, or authorise its publication or display, if the advertisement indicates that a person intends to act in a way that contravenes the Act."

Carefully worded selection criteria should govern eligibility for appointment. Some Christian schools take the view that being a practising Christian is an inherent requirement for all roles within the school. Others just have a strong preference for appointing practising Christians, particularly in teaching roles. Even when being a Christian is not specified as an essential requirement, the Christian ethos of the school can be conveyed by indicating that it is important to the school that teachers understand, and are committed to, Christian education. There should be appropriate questions about this in the application form. Most people considering applying for a position will make their own decision about whether they fit what the school is looking for and whether they would feel comfortable working in that environment.

Where jobs are advertised, it is important to keep sufficient records in relation to decisions about why a particular candidate was chosen while others who applied were not, in terms of their all-round suitability for the position. A multitude of factors go into any employment decision when there is a pool of qualified and capable candidates.

Selecting staff wisely will minimize grief later on, but Christian ministries sometimes find that changes in a staff member's beliefs or values lead to difficulties that were not there, or not apparent, at the time of employment. Such issues won't always result in the school being uncomfortable with the employee remaining; but where it does, the employee may also recognize that he or she will be happier seeking a position elsewhere. Whatever the situation, the school's Christian responsibility is to try to resolve the issue peaceably, maintaining respect for the person involved, and seeking to preserve mutual goodwill. The New Testament letter of James contains a passage on the meaning of heavenly wisdom. One of its attributes is that it is "peace-loving". James concludes: "Peacemakers who sow in peace reap a harvest of righteousness" (Jas 3:17–18).

Jesus' teaching in the Sermon on the Mount is relevant here. He tells his disciples, "if anyone wants to sue you and take your shirt, hand over your coat as well" (Matt 5:40). Of course, we should manage the finances of a church or ministry wisely, but Jesus is saying in this passage that money isn't everything. We can surprise people by being generous. If someone sues us for our shirt, the maximum remedy they can expect is that the judge awards them the shirt. To offer more than this is profoundly countercultural, but it fits with Jesus' teaching to hold lightly to wealth and to trust God for our finances.

Keep calm and carry on giving a Christlike witness

Peter wrote:

> Always be prepared to give an answer to everyone who asks you to give the reason for the hope that you have. But do this with gentleness and respect. (1 Pet 3:15)

How we engage on controversial issues that relate to our beliefs is critical to our witness.

In June 2022, Bethlehem College, a Christian school in Tauranga, New Zealand, found itself in a perfect storm of controversy which began when an LGBTQ+ activist protested its Statement of Belief. This had been amended to state:

> Marriage is an institution created by God in which one man and one woman enter into an exclusive relationship intended for life, and that marriage is the only form of partnership approved by God for sexual relations.

Parents at the school are asked to sign the document to acknowledge that these are the beliefs held by the organization that runs it. The activist criticized the belief on marriage as "discriminatory" and against the law, since New Zealand law enables couples to marry a same-sex partner.[15] The school responded to a press inquiry by saying that the statement was not intended to tell anyone what they are required to believe, but to "transparently explain what we believe".

That was the beginning of a succession of adverse media reports.

15   C Olivier and E Houpt, 'Tauranga's Bethlehem College criticised for "discriminatory" marriage belief', *Bay of Plenty Times*, 11 June 2022 (nzherald.co.nz/bay-of-plenty-times/news/taurangas-bethlehem-college-criticised-for-discriminatory-marriage-belief/ACKCSXMNTDGQ5CRCLF7AMTWZXY).

An unfortunate incident occurred a day or two later when some students took part in an International Day of Silence against bullying. Media reported at the time that students showing support for the LGBTQ+ community received death threats and verbal attacks, including chants of "kill the gays". Students attending the event claimed their phones had been confiscated in order to prevent them recording video footage. These were serious allegations.

The school launched an investigation immediately. It examined CCTV footage and interviewed students, and found that there had been bad behaviour: two pieces of fruit had been thrown, hitting one of the protesters, and offensive comments were made. The school took disciplinary action against these offenders. However, its investigation also concluded that there were no chants of "kill the gays" as alleged. The school made clear in its public statement that it does not tolerate bullying, and expects its students to show civility and tolerance for differing views. It also explained that the reason two students' phones were confiscated was that their use breached the school's standard 'no phones during school hours' policy.[16]

The next day, the press reported that another activist, who had launched an online petition calling for an independent investigation into allegations of "abuse" at the school, claimed to have received 'hundreds' of online messages from past and current students alleging negative experiences at the school. This activist claimed that "a pattern emerged of alleged experiences of sexism, racism, homophobia, transphobia, ableism and other forms of discrimination".[17] So, within three days of the original media story concerning a protest against the school's mainstream Christian views on sex and marriage, the school was being publicly accused of all manner

16 A Quill, 'School launches investigation after alleged threats made to students supporting LGBTQIA+ community', *Stuff*, 13 June 2022 (stuff.co.nz/bay-of-plenty/ 300611407/school-launch-investigation-after-alleged-threats-made-to-students-supporting-lgbtqia-community).

17 C Olivier and E Houpt, 'Bethlehem College: Petition calls for independent investigation into alleged "abuse" at the school', *The New Zealand Herald*, 14 June 2022 (nzherald. co.nz/nz/bethlehem-college-petition-calls-for-independent-investigation-into-alleged-abuse-at-the-school/JXDXXNZZCJSQULSOYRREWUAXQY).

of discrimination and poor conduct—on an industrial scale. It also faced calls for an inquiry by the Education Review Office (ERO), which might have threatened its accreditation.

The Chair of the Trustees responded to this story by indicating that he had not received complaints about such matters, but he encouraged those with concerns to contact the school and speak to the counsellors. He said the school did not discriminate and did not tolerate bullying. He said the school taught students to understand and respect people with differing views, faiths and backgrounds. He also made it clear that complaints would be dealt with in an open and honest manner, with "care to preserve relationships, grace, forgiveness and love".[18]

The pile-on continued in the following days, with stories about a draft policy on gender identity and an account of a student who identified as transgender who was not permitted to change name or gender identification at school. The Minister for Education and the Prime Minister both commented on the issues publicly, with the Prime Minister saying "serious concerns" had been raised about the school.[19] The Ministry of Education required the school to remove its statement about marriage and commenced an investigation focused upon the emotional safety of LGBTQ+ students.

The school dealt with this firestorm with support from a Christian communications expert and a lawyer. Such guidance is often invaluable in situations like this. The school had various choices about how to respond to the mounting tide of criticism. It could have been defensive or aggressive; it could have apologized profusely and capitulated on its statement concerning sex and marriage; it could have hidden behind 'no comment' responses. Or it could have engaged with all the issues publicly, maintaining a Christlike tone in communications.

The school chose the last of these options, calmly rebutting

18 Quoted in Olivier and Houpt, 'Bethlehem College'.
19 'Bethlehem College: Prime Minister Jacinda Ardern acknowledges "serious concerns" raised about school', *The New Zealand Herald*, 21 June 2022 (nzherald. co.nz/nz/bethlehem-college-prime-minister-jacinda-ardern-acknowledges-serious-concerns-raised-about-school/FLXBZJMBOOHOTKMKWFFMMCUCRE).

allegations that appeared, on investigation, to be false or without substance, and reiterating its commitment to a safe environment for all students. The school emphasized that it taught students to respond to people with different views in a respectful way, and it modelled this in its own communications. The school's message was that it respected the views of its critics and asked them to show the same respect for its beliefs. When a mother and daughter (not associated with the school) started a daily protest at the school gates, staff took them coffee each morning. The school also informed the media that it supported people's right to protest.[20]

In the midst of this storm, various claims were made that the school's stance on marriage violated New Zealand law. This is quite a common claim from activists who are no doubt sincere but not legally trained. The school checked its position legally and rebutted the allegation. A secular law that permits same-sex couples to marry says nothing about what Christians should believe concerning marriage.

The June 2022 publicity was not the end of the school's problems. An ERO report in December 2023 found that, while many students, staff and parents reported that the school provides a positive educational experience, a strong sense of community for learners, and a safe learning environment, this was not the experience of all students. A small number of current and former students reported feeling deeply hurt by their experiences at the school. These students believed they had been specifically singled out and subjected to bullying and targeted because of their sexual orientation.[21] ERO concluded: "The school has yet to fully develop a culture that characterizes respect, embraces diversity, and provides safety for all students".[22] While the report made carefully phrased criticisms,

---

20 C Olivier and E Houpt, 'Pride protest at Bethlehem College over its gender and marriage stance', *Bay of Plenty Times*, 25 June 2022 (nzherald.co.nz/bay-of-plenty-times/news/pride-protest-at-bethlehem-college-over-its-gender-and-marriage-stance/72OZQR4IJBOJDMVHY25WBSNN44).

21 Education Review Office, 'Bethlehem College', Education Review Office website, 12 December 2023 (ero.govt.nz/institution/77/bethlehem-college).

22 Education Review Office, 'Bethlehem College'.

evidence did not support the very serious allegations made in the press in 2022.

Issues concerning marriage, same-sex attraction and gender identity continue to be challenges for Christian schools seeking to hold traditional beliefs on these issues while providing an inclusive and caring environment for all students. How they respond to adverse publicity requires considerable wisdom, as well as calm refutation of unsubstantiated claims. There needs to be a strong emphasis on love and care for all students, recognizing that students will go through a journey of exploring their identity, sexuality, beliefs and moral values during their time at school, and may continue on that journey well into their adult years. They must eventually reach mature decisions on such matters for themselves.

The Christian school should, of course, explain the Bible's teaching on marriage, sexuality and gender where relevant to the life of the school. But it can do so while also presenting itself as a safe and respectful environment in which to explore these issues in an age-appropriate way. This is in stark contrast to many state schools in which teachers and administrators press children to explore issues of sexuality and gender identity in ways that are neither age-appropriate nor that allow room for the students to hold different moral, cultural or religious values.

Understood in this way, it is the Christian school that is typically more tolerant than the state school, and that provides a more accepting environment for students of different faiths and cultures to come to their own decisions on these matters without being exposed prematurely to adult issues and concepts. Some state schools are very unsafe environments for children who may become confused about their gender as a result of the unscientific ideas they are taught.[23] This is one reason why in Australia and elsewhere, there is a flight to faith-based schools or to home education.

---

23   P Parkinson, 'Gender Identity Discrimination and Religious Freedom', *Journal of Law and Religion*, 2023, 38(1):10–37 (doi.org/10.1017/jlr.2022.45).

Negotiate appropriate compromises with regulators

This chapter has focused largely on the issues facing Christian schools that hold to traditional theological positions in a society that does not share those positions. But these issues are just a subset of the clashes occurring between Christian values and an increasingly secular culture. Such issues will continue to cause debates and conflict in churches and between Church and State. The goalposts of acceptable sexual conduct keep moving.

Governments in multicultural societies must grapple with how to manage a diversity of opinion. For example, while in many countries the law has changed to allow same-sex marriage, governments have to recognize that a large proportion of the population may hold religious beliefs about the nature of marriage that are incongruent with secular values. To forbid religious organizations to maintain their beliefs and values is another form of discrimination.

Because governments and regulatory bodies must, like churches, navigate the sensitivities of a multicultural society without imposing secular beliefs on religious bodies, there will sometimes be room for negotiation on how to deal with these issues. In some cases, this may involve a 'don't ask, don't tell' approach in which governments and regulators accept that a religious organization funded by it to provide much-needed community services is not able to comply with all of the government's normal funding requirements. The government could at any time withdraw the funding; the religious organization could at any time withdraw the services. Neither wants that. Making a conflict public by drawing lines in the sand will often not be in anyone's best interests, least of all the vulnerable people who rely on those services.

When conflicts occur with regulators, or there is potential for conflict, it may often be possible to negotiate compromise positions—a carefully worded addition to the website here, a deletion there. Often, little is lost from agreeing to modest changes. Regulators will feel bound to insist on certain positions and interpretations of the law if challenged directly, but confrontation with a religious body may not otherwise be a high priority. Governments also will be sensitive to possible electoral implications if they engage in a war on people of faith, particularly if their MPs are in constituencies with a large number of religious adherents. It may well be possible to negotiate face-saving compromises in such circumstances.

Lines in the sand

There will, of course, sometimes need to be lines drawn in the sand. One of the most difficult issues that Christian organizations may face is whether to withdraw entirely from the provision of community services on behalf of a government. If a Christian organization is no longer permitted to be Christian, or governments do not respect their right to refuse to cooperate with abortion or euthanasia practices, is there any point in continuing to provide government-funded services?

Governments rely heavily upon faith-based organizations to deliver community services to the disadvantaged, to offer aged care, and in some cases to provide hospitals and other health services. From a government's perspective, the outsourcing of service delivery to non-profit organizations has numerous benefits. They take all the risk in providing staff with continuing paid employment and in providing infrastructure for the service. The government can withdraw the funds if its priorities change, or if it prefers to go with another provider. This leaves the organization with the cost of buildings, redundancy payments and more. If governments had to provide directly all the community services that they fund faith-based groups to deliver, it is likely that this would come at a cost both to quality and efficiency. It therefore remains in the best interests of government not to drive faith-based organizations out of service delivery.

However, should the need arise, the time may come when Christian organizations conclude that their resources are better allocated elsewhere. This would mean that government funding will be rejected.

For now, we are not in that place. Withdrawal from providing community services is the 'nuclear option'. It is a card that can only be played once,[24] and we should avoid idle threats to play it. However, we must draw our lines in the sand long before we have to cross them. Withdrawing services would bring considerable difficulty and distress to those that rely on God's people for services, and who would not be equally satisfied by having that service provided by some other organization.

24   A point made by Archbishop Anthony Fisher in 'Religious freedom in a secular world: Doomed or doable?', *Catholic Archdiocese of Sydney*, 31 May 2024 (sydneycatholic. org/addresses-and-statements/2024/religious-freedom-in-a-secular-world-doomed-or-doable-31-may-2024).

9

A CONFLICT WITH CHRIST'S COMMANDS

How do we decide when not to comply with the law?

In a previous chapter, we have seen how both in the Bible itself, and in the teachings of the church's greatest theologians through the centuries, there has been a consistent tension between recognition that government is given by God, and the notion that the government's licence is limited. God both authorizes governments and limits their role. If we are forced to a choice between obedience to law and obedience to God, the choice ought to be clear in principle: "We must obey God rather than human beings!" (Acts 5:29).

As Christians, we ought to have great respect for law, strive to obey it where we know its requirements, and understand that governments—even those with which we disagree on many matters—are ordained by God. We are to be law-abiding because God wishes this, not merely from fear of the consequences of not being law-abiding. We are to be good citizens of the country in which we live.

However, we also have another citizenship. Paul states it very simply: "our citizenship is in heaven" (Phil 3:20). And while we give to Caesar what is Caesar's, we also give to God what is God's (Mark 12:17). We have no obligation to support Caesar when he overreaches his legitimate authority.

How and when we exercise the choice to disobey a law is another matter, for that choice can be exercised in a variety of different ways, depending on the circumstances. It can be exercised quietly or openly. It may involve substantial, but not complete, compliance with the law. It may involve deliberately and openly breaching the law as a public protest to try to have the law changed. It is, of course, a Christian option to defend oneself or an organization through the courts, challenging the interpretation of the law or running a legitimate defence to its application.

Here are some principles that can help guide us in what are likely to be difficult and consequential decisions.

Affirm what we can

Even when we might have a conflict with some aspects of a law, or at least some difficulty in knowing how to comply with it, we may be able to affirm much of its spirit and intent.

Discrimination law is an example. Equality is a profoundly Christian concept, and one not found in pre-Christian societies such as ancient Rome. When Paul wrote in Galatians that "there is neither Jew nor Greek, neither slave nor free, nor is there male and female, for you are all one in Christ Jesus" (Gal 3:28), he was expounding a quite revolutionary doctrine (see also Rom 10:12). He referred to the most fundamental divisions and categorizations of the Roman world that rendered people unequal and said that in Christ, by way of contrast, all are equal.

Jesus also had a revolutionary approach to those he met. There is a constant theme in the Gospels of people criticizing Jesus for the company he kept. This is because he modelled the very best form of non-discrimination. He did not discriminate against tax collectors (Luke 19:1–10), and he ate with people whom the Pharisees labelled as sinners and with whom they thought Jesus should not associate (Matt 9:10–12). He allowed a 'sinful woman', most likely a prostitute, to wet his feet with her tears and to wipe them with her hair before pouring perfume on them. His devoutly religious host was horrified (Luke 7:36–50).

As Christians, we can affirm all non-discrimination laws to the extent that we believe that all human beings are equal in the eyes of God. It is not consistent with Christ's life and teaching to ill-treat people. We can affirm all anti-vilification laws to the extent that they prohibit stirring up hatred or violence against people because of their race, religion, political beliefs, or other characteristics. So even where we have difficulties with aspects of the law, we can still affirm the good purposes of the law insofar as this is consistent with our beliefs.

However, there are applications of some anti-discrimination laws with which we may well not be able to agree. Christians schools, for example, are unlikely to accept that the staffing profile of the school should look no different from the state school next door. They don't want a right to discriminate in a negative sense; but they want the right to select staff who share the mission of the school. Christians may also have difficulties with some anti-vilification laws that are so widely drafted that people can claim a legal remedy just because they find certain views 'offensive'. Such laws are far too easily weaponized by activists wanting to shut down certain points of view. Our affirmation of anti-discrimination laws and laws about not causing offence can only go so far.

Limit cooperation with those who enforce unjust laws

If a police officer or a government regulator asks us directly whether we are engaging in conduct that may breach the law, how are we to respond? This was an issue for couriers carrying Bibles and Christian books into Russia and Eastern Europe during the communist era. A typical question at the border might have been: "Are you carrying any Bibles or pornography?" How should the Christian courier at the border respond?

There is a curious passage in the Gospel of John that may offer some assistance with an issue of this kind. Jesus was urged by his brothers to go up to Jerusalem for the Festival of Tabernacles. The reason they gave was that if he wanted to be a public figure, he needed to go where the people were rather than hiding in the back-woods of the Galilee region. "No one who wants to become a public figure acts in secret", they said (John 7:4). That might have been well-meaning advice from a disciple; but John makes clear that at this stage, Jesus' brothers were not believers, and so had very little understanding of his mission and purpose (v 5).[1] A few verses later, John records what Jesus tells his brothers: "You go to the festival. I am not going up to this festival, because my time has not yet fully come" (v 8). However, after his brothers had left for the festival, Jesus went also, in secret (v 10). Can this be reconciled with what he told his brothers?

Some translations of verse 8 insert the word 'yet' so that the verse reads: "I am not going up to this festival yet".[2] That might be a reasonable interpretation of Jesus' meaning. Either way, he is not lying to his brothers; he is telling them that he will go to the Feast on his heavenly Father's timing, not on his (then) unbelieving brothers' timing. But the point for our purposes is that his words appear to have been ambiguous: he didn't offer his brothers a full explanation of his intentions. They might well have been very surprised to have found him teaching in the temple courts halfway through the festival (v 14).

Jesus responded similarly to others who did not have the best of motives in asking questions. For example, he refused to engage with the chief priests and elders who questioned his authority (Matt 21:23–27). In Matthew 22, it is recorded that the Pharisees sent people to Jesus seeking to trap him with a question, asking him whether it is right to pay the imperial tax to Caesar. The question was laden with political meaning. What was Jesus' attitude to the Roman occupation of Palestine? Did he support a refusal to pay taxes? The question sought a direct answer. Jesus responded to the question with a question: whose head was on the coin used to pay taxes? The questioners had their answer (Matt 22:15–21).

---

1   After the resurrection, this changed. Remarkably, Jesus' brothers and his mother were recorded as being among the disciples praying together in the Upper Room after Jesus had ascended into heaven (Acts 1:14). That was a transformation from their earlier attitudes towards his ministry (Mark 3:21, 31; 6:1–4).

2   Some ancient manuscripts contain the Greek word for 'not yet' (*oupō*), while others contain the word for 'not' (*ouk*). The latter is more likely, but the substance of the verse's meaning does not change either way.

We don't always need to respond to inquiries with a fulsome response. There may be cases where a non-answer or a response that evades the trap set is the most sensible way of responding.

'Conversion therapy' laws, discussed in chapter 3, provide an illustration. The *Change or Suppression (Conversion) Practices Prohibition Act 2021* in Victoria is among the most extreme of these laws. While the law doesn't necessarily target Christians, it is explicit about referencing a "prayer based practice" as one of the prohibited practices. Guidance from the Victorian Equal Opportunity and Human Rights Commission on how to interpret the legislation implies that people of faith could be threatened with jail for praying with someone, at their request, about an unwanted same-sex attraction or distress about their inner sense of gender identity. It offers examples of what it claims are illegal practices under the legislation, including a religious leader "using a youth group session to provide 'support' through group prayer to a young person to help them fight a desire to act on their feelings of same-sex attraction".[3] Of course, a young person who seeks to remain obedient to a Christian view of sex before marriage might equally seek prayer from a trusted group not to act on their heterosexual attraction if they are experiencing a lot of sexual temptation. That, too, seems to be forbidden by Victorian law, which defines sexual orientation to include both same-sex and heterosexual attraction, and makes it unlawful to try to help someone 'suppress' that attraction.

The Commission has various powers under the Act to seek information from people or organizations. If a complaint is made to it, alleging a change or suppression practice, the Commission may ask the person or organization about which the complaint is made to provide further information that the Commission considers necessary to determine its response. Compliance with such a request is voluntary at this stage. In response to a complaint of this kind, the Commission has various options, including doing nothing, adopting

3   See the 'Examples of prohibited practices' tab at 'For people of faith, professionals and other communities', *Victorian Equal Opportunity and Human Rights Commission* (humanrights.vic.gov.au/change-or-suppression-practices/for-professionals-institutions-and-communities).

an educational approach, facilitating a mediated outcome, or refer-ring the matter to prosecutors.[4]

The Commission can open a formal investigation if it considers there is "an issue that is serious in nature or indicates change or suppression practices that are systemic or persisting".[5] If it decides to open an investigation, then it does have coercive powers. It may issue a written notice that requires the person to provide infor-mation or a document. It may also compel attendance to answer questions. An individual or organization can be fined for failing to do so.[6]

How then should a church respond to an initial request for infor-mation from the Commission that says it has had a report that the church is engaging in change or suppression practices? The church could choose not to respond. That is within its legal rights. Or it could give the kind of less-than-fulsome response that Jesus gave to his brothers. If the allegation is that members of the youth group prayed for someone in the group who asked for prayer to manage a same-sex attraction, a response might be to send a very brief but polite reply the effect that the church does not encourage practices that seek to change or suppress the sexual orientation or gender identity of the person. That uses the exact language of the legis-lation itself, without engaging with any specifics of the allegation, including whether members of the youth group prayed for the indi-vidual, or what they prayed for.

Such a courteous but limited response could be regarded as entirely truthful on several bases. First, it may well be entirely correct that the church does not *encourage* change or suppression practices. Second, we may take the view that the law, properly interpreted, is concerned with discredited practices of 'conversion therapy' that use therapeutic processes to try to change a person's sexual orientation. Arguably, it was not intended to be interpreted so broadly, particularly given that the human right of religious

4   *Change or Suppression (Conversion) Practices Prohibition Act 2021*, s 24–32.
5   *Change or Suppression (Conversion) Practices Prohibition Act 2021*, s 34.
6   *Change or Suppression (Conversion) Practices Prohibition Act 2021*, s 36–38.

freedom is protected in Victoria's Charter of Rights.[7]

Third, the church may legitimately argue that praying for someone at their request to maintain their religious commitment to celibacy is hardly praying for them to suppress their *sexual orientation*; rather, it is praying that God would help them to suppress *acting upon* it in a way which is inconsistent with Christian teaching. It is an ordinary aspect of human experience to experience sexual attraction. By choosing not to act upon every attraction we experience, even if we have the opportunity to do so, we are not suppressing our sexual orientation; we are simply keeping our attraction within bounds—for good reasons.

In responding to an inquiry of this kind, there is no point getting into an argument with the Commission if it is committed to an entirely different worldview on sexual ethics. We do not owe the Commission any explanation concerning our view on when, or why, celibacy is a Christian calling.

What if a formal investigation is launched and a written notice is sent requiring information to be provided? If a church leader decides not to comply at all, he or she risks a fine. However, there is a legal right to remain silent. Section 39 of the Act provides:

> It is a reasonable excuse for a natural person to refuse to give information, answer a question or produce a document under this Act if the giving of the information, the answering of the question or the production of the document would tend to incriminate the person.

The church or its leader could invoke that right. Alternatively, the leader could respond by providing answers. Again, those answers need not be fulsome. When lawyers prepare witnesses for cross-examination in court, the standard advice is to give yes or no answers where possible. Don't volunteer any information. The

---

7   Section 14(1) of the *Charter of Human Rights and Responsibilities Act 2006* provides that every person, including a child or young person, has the right to freedom of religion, which includes the freedom to demonstrate that person's religion or belief in worship, observance, practice and teaching, either individually or as part of a community, in public or in private.

cross-examiner is not your friend, and you should assume they are not trying to be fair or reasonable. It may be wise to make the same assumption about regulators, individual police officers, or other enforcement authorities.

A brief answer can create its own helpful ambiguities. Consider again the question asked at the border of communist Eastern Europe: "Do you have Bibles or pornography?" Even if the car is full of Bibles, to answer "no" may well be truthful (because there is no pornography in the car), if not complete. An answer of "yes, I have my personal Bible in my suitcase", is also truthful, if not complete. In situations where a truthful answer to a direct question could put you, or someone else, in danger, there is an ethical problem, for "the belt of truth" is part of our spiritual armour (Eph 6:14), and truth is not lightly to be discarded. However, the Bible does at least give us the example of Rahab. She protected Joshua's spies by giving an untruthful response to the king of Jericho's men who were searching for them (Josh 2:1–7), and she is highly commended in the New Testament (Heb 11:31; Jas 2:25).

In summary, when dealing with those who seek to enforce laws that impact adversely on Christian living or ministry, we should be polite to them as individuals, and co-operative to the extent possible, for typically they are only doing their job. However, wisdom in these situations may require a brief, ambiguous or less-than-fulsome answer. We risk difficulties if, naively, we feel the need to tell someone the complete truth about a matter when their job is to enforce laws that unreasonably restrict religious freedom.

Choose whether non-compliance will be quiet or open

Non-violent civil disobedience has a long tradition as a form of protest, and some people may feel a moral responsibility to engage in this form of protest. As the great liberal philosopher John Rawls argued, civil disobedience must be done in public, or it is not legitimately a form of protest (see chapter 6).

If disobedience is for the purposes of protest, then punishment is an expected consequence, although the police and prosecutorial authorities may choose not to respond in this way so as not to aggravate the situation. Sometimes mass protests can bring down governments, as they did in Eastern Europe in 1989. People joined these protests without worrying too much whether the government had given its permission for the assembly.

The alternative to open civil disobedience is simply quiet non-compliance. Because governments rely so heavily on voluntary compliance with laws, quiet non-compliance may be an effective way of responding to an unjust law. Governments, unable to rely on voluntary compliance, must then decide what resources and political capital they want to put into enforcing it. It may not be worth the effort and political cost to try to uphold a law that has very little public support and that involves open confrontation with otherwise law-abiding and productive citizens.

Quiet non-compliance is the default option for living under oppressive regimes. There is no need to draw attention to religious activities of which the government may disapprove. When you live under an oppressive regime, theological arguments about the duty to obey the law have a different hue. It may not be possible to live an authentic Christian life without breaking the law, or at least arousing the ire of the government.

Discern what is a Christian cause

Peter instructed his readers:

> If you suffer, it should not be as a murderer or thief or any other kind of criminal, or even as a meddler. However, if you suffer as a Christian, do not be ashamed, but praise God that you bear that name. (1 Pet 4:15–16)

The contrast between being punished as a murderer and a thief or as a Christian ought to be a very clear one; but sometimes it is more difficult to discern when disobedience to law is required or justified out of obedience to Christ.

The Covid lockdowns around the world gave rise to various challenges of this kind. Looking back on how governments responded to the sudden emergence of this dangerous pandemic, we might well identify various decisions that were unwise, that involved an unnecessary restriction on civil liberties, or that were based on poor-quality information. However, hindsight is always 20/20. Amid a public-health crisis the like of which had not been seen for a century, governments typically did their best with the use of broad prohibitions and controls.

Those controls suppressed religious liberty as they suppressed other liberties. One argument put for disobeying the public-health edicts was that Scripture urges us not to refrain from meeting together (Heb 10:25). Who knows whether the writer of Hebrews would have thought that meeting on Zoom during a public-health emergency was a sufficient way to meet together in the circumstances? The New Testament is not a comprehensive manual for Christian living in all the modern circumstances of the 21st century, and there is room for legitimate disagreement on the application of biblical principles to novel situations of this kind.

To the extent that these were consistently applied public-health measures, they were not intended to suppress religious freedom; they had a broad secular justification. Early in the pandemic, when the scale and seriousness of the problem were not yet understood, some churches and other religious groups were thought to be epicentres for the spread of the virus, leading to many deaths.[8] Long after the dangers of the virus were understood, and its means of transmission identified, some churches considered it their Christian duty to defy the public-health requirements.[9] Maybe they thought the biblical justification for so doing was compelling; but an alternative view is that in keeping their churches open, they put their members, as well as the broader community, at unnecessary risk of death or serious illness.

---

8   This was the case, for example in South Korea: see EJ Smith 'Why churches are the source of South Korea's major COVID-19 outbreaks', *SBS News*, 19 August 2020 (sbs.com.au/news/dateline/article/why-churches-are-the-source-of-south-koreas-major-covid-19-outbreaks/cnolpj3mq).
9   For a view that disobedience to the Covid lockdown laws was the right option, see N Busenitz & J Coates, *God vs. Government: Taking a biblical stand when Christ and compliance collide*, Harvest House, 2022.

Christian pastors did not have a better understanding of the science at the time than the public-health authorities, nor did they possess a better judgement about the respective costs and benefits of mass lockdowns. In retrospect, it may well have been better not to have closed schools or to have imposed such severe restrictions on the rights of other people who were at a relatively low risk of serious illness. But it is at least arguable that civil authorities made good-faith judgements on the basis of what they knew at the relevant times.

The demonstrations that involved incursions into the US Capitol on January 6, 2021 raise similar issues. There is no mistaking the Christian identification of many Trump supporters who marched, demonstrated and rioted that day. As the *Washington Post* reported: "Images and references to being on the march for Jesus were common at the massive Jan. 6 rally".[10] No doubt those who attended this public gathering had a range of motivations. For some, it was only a public protest to show support for President Trump and his claim that the election result was achieved fraudulently, even though these claims had been rejected by the Department of Justice and the courts. Many, no doubt, did not go to Washington, DC expecting to engage in a forcible entry of the Capitol.

Others, however, clearly did intend this. A reporter for *The New Yorker* magazine recorded video footage of some demonstrators who forced their way into the building past an outnumbered police force.[11] As they walked the corridors, they shouted over and over, "treason!" and "defend the Constitution!". Some then found a door that gave them entry into the Senate chamber, which had been evacuated only a few minutes before. One leader, dressed in military fatigues and helmet, urged the rioters to behave respectfully towards the place. This was an "information operation", he explained. Others were in no mood for orderly protest. One said, "while we're here, we might as well set up a government".

10 M Boorstein, 'For some Christians, the Capitol riot doesn't change the prophecy: Trump will be president', *Washington Post*, 14 January 2021 (washingtonpost.com/religion/2021/01/14/prophets-apostles-christian-prophesy-trump-won-biden-capitol).

11 The New Yorker, 'A Reporter's Footage from Inside the Capitol Siege' [video], *YouTube*, 17 January 2021 (youtube.com/watch?v=270F8s5TEKY).

For several minutes they rummaged through the Senators' papers and speech notes, looking for material to use against them. In the gallery, a bare-chested man chanted, howled and banged his American flag on the ground. He was wearing a horned bearskin headdress and patriotic face paint. Then he came down to the floor of the Senate chamber and sat in the Senate President's chair, saying that Vice-President Mike Pence was a traitor.

He was joined at the front of the Senate chamber by three other men. One of them yelled "Jesus Christ, we invoke your name!" to loud cheers. The man with the horned bearskin headdress then led them all in a lengthy and fervent prayer, thanking God for filling the Senate chamber with patriots and for allowing the United States to be 'reborn'. The assembled group of young men joined in, heads bowed solemnly, hands raised in invocation to God. Then they left peacefully, expressing their support for the police, who escorted them out. The horned bearskin man, Jacob Chansley, pleaded guilty to a felony and was sentenced to 41 months in prison in 2021.[12]

Were the activities in which Christians engaged on January 6 really in pursuit of a Christian cause? Clearly, their cause was a political one. They supported one candidate for the presidency over another, to the extent of engaging in actions that were intended, in some way, to affect the Senate's certification of the election results that day. Some American Christians may have believed strongly in that cause, but it is important to be clear that it was not a Christian cause. As Psalm 146:3 says, we are not to "put [our] trust in princes, in human beings who cannot save". It is a grave error to associate the purposes of the Creator of the universe with the position of a political party in one country at one moment in time. Political parties take different positions on the equality/liberty spectrum as well as on the proper scope for public services and the redistribution of wealth within a society. Various major parties in modern democracies have emphases within their policy frameworks that Christians, informed by Jesus' teaching, could readily endorse.

12 At the commencement of President Trump's second term, Chansley was pardoned after serving his sentence, as were almost all those charged with offences on that day.

Jesus gave no indication that his cause and his kingdom could be directly identified with any earthly political leader. We should therefore be very cautious about claiming that our *political* cause is a *Christian* cause.

Testing claims of a Christian cause

A number of questions might be asked when seeking to determine whether it is right to disobey the law, either overtly or quietly.

Can we live our lives in a godly way?

First, does the law impede the right of Christians to "live peaceful and quiet lives in all godliness and holiness", as Paul instructed us to pray for (1 Tim 2:1–4)? A law which purports to prevent Christians praying together, such as the conversion therapy law in Victoria, would seem to impede ordinary Christian living. If the law were focused only on coercive conduct towards a vulnerable person (where that conduct included prayer purporting to cure someone of their same-sex attraction), and such law were narrowly construed with proper respect for freedom of religion, it would be different.

Is evangelism restricted?

Second, does the law impede the right of Christians to share the gospel? This is the context in which Peter and the other apostles told the Sanhedrin that they had to obey God rather than human beings (Acts 5:29).

This is not to say that we should disobey any and every law that impedes freedom to share the gospel. For example, there may be legitimate restrictions on when and in what manner Christians can engage in street preaching in a public location—constraints that apply equally to other forms of public speech.[13] There may also be constraints imposed by state education authorities that allow

13 See, for example, *Attorney-General for South Australia v Corporation of the City of Adelaide and Ors* [2013] HCA 3. In this case, the High Court of Australia upheld a city by-law that restricted preaching, canvassing, haranguing and handing out printed matter in a pedestrian shopping precinct in Adelaide.

chaplains to work in state schools on the condition that they do not proselytize students. Where a person accepts an offer of employment under these conditions, it is right to honour the agreement.

That said, the Christian's default stance towards government restrictions on evangelism should be, at the very least, deep unease. We must keep returning to Peter and John's words when they were threatened: "We must obey God rather than human beings!" What's more, there are countries where the Christian faith is severely restricted and governments typically impose much more far-reaching constraints upon any sharing of the gospel. In those situations, Christians are not bound to obey such laws—although, of course, we take risks when we breach them. Even at the time of Acts 5, Peter and John were very familiar with these risks. Given that one ended his life in exile and one was crucified upside-down (according to tradition), the risks only became worse as they went along.

Is there Christian consensus?
Third, is the law seen as an impediment to Christian living or witness by a substantial proportion of faithful Christians, and in particular by theologically educated Christian leaders of high standing? We may have all kinds of views as individuals about what Jesus would do in a given circumstance, or what Christian living requires when facing a particular decision about obedience to the law. However, humility, as well as church discipline and order, should lead us to ask whether our understanding of our faith is widely shared in the Christian community. We need to be wary of fringe beliefs that are not part of the Christian consensus.

In 2022, an eight-year-old girl who was diabetic died in Toowoomba, Queensland, after her father stopped giving her insulin injections. The girl's parents and older brother, and the leader of the fringe 'church' to which they belonged, together with ten other members of the congregation, were convicted of manslaughter in January 2025 and all sentenced to lengthy jail terms.[14] They had all

---

14   L Lavelle & T Siganto, 'Religious group members found guilty of manslaughter of eight-year-old Elizabeth Struhs', *ABC News*, 29 January 2025 (abc.net.au/news/2025-01-29/elizabeth-struhs-diabetes-insulin-witheld-verdict/104863074).

been active participants in helping to 'care' for the girl and praying for her healing, while supporting the parents' decision not to give her insulin or seek other medical treatment. The mother had previously been jailed for this, trusting only in God's power to heal.[15] The child's death occurred three weeks after the mother returned home from prison. Group members believed that the child would be raised from the dead.

Nothing can stop a little group of sincere believers forming their own 'church' and creating their own set of doctrines, including rejection of doctors and medical treatment. However, none of the defendants could reasonably claim that, when sentenced to prison, they are suffering "as a Christian" (1 Pet 4:16). As individual Christians, or even small groups of believers, we are not entitled to claim that beliefs that few other Christians share, and which are not grounded in any mainstream theological interpretation of the New Testament, are authentically Christian beliefs.

Is the concern about the law because of a conflict with faith?

Fourth, are the objections to the law based upon Christian teaching, or on some other valid but non-religious consideration? One of the issues that caused significant conflicts between Christians during the Covid pandemic concerned vaccine mandates. There are strong arguments for saying that requiring people to be vaccinated as a condition of maintaining their employment or attending a church service is a violation of the right to determine what they do with their bodies. It is a basic principle of medical practice that the patient must give an informed consent to treatment, except in an emergency where the patient is unable to provide that consent. That principle of bodily autonomy applies to vaccinations. On the other hand, if public-health authorities assumed at the time that being unvaccinated involved a greater risk both of contracting and spreading the illness, then there were legitimate public-health concerns that might reasonably have justified requiring vaccination for

15   T Siganto, 'Elizabeth Struhs's mother previously told jury her daughter's illness was "given by God"', *ABC News*, 18 July 2024 (abc.net.au/news/2024-07-18/elizabeth-struhs-murder-trial-religious-group-toowoomba/104114306).

some occupations, particularly in health services and aged care.

On this issue, many considerations needed to be explored carefully. The first was whether the circumstances in which the vaccines were created or tested made it unethical for Christians to take them. An argument was put against certain Covid vaccines on the basis that they may have been developed and produced from cell lines derived from two aborted foetuses in the last century. The Vatican's Congregation for the Doctrine of the Faith took a leadership role on this issue. It categorized such a connection as "remote", and said that consequently there is no ethical objection to taking a vaccine that might have such a link somewhere in its developmental history.[16]

There might have been numerous other concerns about the vaccines, including how quickly they were developed, whether they were adequately tested in that timeframe, and whether there had been sufficient consideration given to the benefits as against the risks, particularly for younger people for whom Covid did not present a severe risk compared to the risk to the elderly. All of these are valid considerations that may have informed the decision of faithful Christians not to receive the vaccine, including very well-informed doctors who considered the available research evidence. Some of them were unable to work in their jobs because of a vaccine mandate.

However, the decision not to receive the vaccine could not easily be considered a religiously based decision unless some stronger religious basis than the remote link to aborted foetuses could be put forward. The Bible itself has nothing to say about vaccines. It certainly gives us no guidance whatsoever on the medical efficacy or benefit of a new vaccine. A religious person who has an objection to a vaccine does not have a religious objection simply because he or she happens to be religious. He or she might have any number of other reasonable objections to the way such mandates were put in place, and it is legitimate for us to have our say on such matters as

16 Congregation for the Doctrine of the Faith, 'Note on the morality of using some anti-Covid-19 vaccines', *The Holy See*, 21 December 2020 (www.vatican.va/roman_curia/congregations/cfaith/documents/rc_con_cfaith_doc_20201221_nota-vaccini-anticovid_en.html).

citizens. But we must be careful to distinguish our reasonable views from those that depend upon divine revelation.

The consequences of disobedience

A choice to disobey the law carries with it a choice to be fined or otherwise punished for a breach of the law, and we cannot complain if that occurs.

Whether or not that happens depends on a variety of factors. When it comes to driving offences, including speeding, consequences are likely to depend on where the police cameras are at the time. We may even be warned specifically, some distance away, that there is a camera in operation.

When it comes to regulatory offences and indeed criminal offences, decision-makers have a great deal of discretion about whether to prosecute or whether to take other action. A police officer stopping a driver for some infraction of the road rules might choose just to give a warning. A regulator might send a letter reminding the person or organization of their obligations. When children and young people commit offences, 'diversion', as it is called, is the default option. That is, police and other authorities will look for ways to avoid a formal prosecution. That might take many forms—working with parents to impose discipline at home, a formal 'caution', referral to drug or alcohol services, or placing a child in out-of-home care if serious abuse or neglect at home is an obvious contributor to the child's offending behaviour.

It is not uncommon at all for prosecutors to drop a case even after the police have laid charges. That decision can be made for a range of different reasons. For example, perhaps the victim, if there is one, no longer wishes to see the alleged offender prosecuted, and so will be a reluctant witness. Perhaps it is not in the best interests of the victim to put him or her through the difficulties of a trial. Perhaps the evidence overall is not strong enough to secure a conviction. Or perhaps there are other reasons why it is not in the public interest to proceed with the prosecution, including that the alleged offender is not a danger to the community, and the risk of reoffending is slight.

A factor that may well play a role in the decision is the availability of prosecutors and courts. In England, for example, the government has faced a perfect storm of problems in maintaining the operation of the criminal-justice system. A 2024 report by the National Audit Office found that, as at the end of 2023, over 67,000 cases were awaiting trial in the Crown Court, which hears the more serious criminal matters. This represents an increase in the backlog of 78 per cent since the end of 2019, due mainly to the Covid pandemic, but also to other factors.[17] A backlog like this is not quickly reduced. Meanwhile, the prison population has reached full capacity, leading to emergency action in July 2024 to release some prisoners after serving as little as 40 per cent of their sentence.[18]

In such circumstances where backlogs are very long, and where people who might eventually be found not guilty are in prison awaiting trial, prosecutors naturally must use sensible judgements about what cases they pursue and what cases they decide not to pursue. They will typically give priority to cases of serious harm to others, such as child sexual abuse, rape, assaults leading to physical injury (in particular, domestic violence), and drug importation.

This is the context in which, as law-abiding Christians, we need to worry about being pursued by prosecutors who weaponize laws as a means of persecution or harassment. It could happen—and it does happen in totalitarian countries. However, in Western democracies where all public services and institutions, including the courts, are under huge pressure from their workloads, ideologically driven prosecutions—for example, those based upon expression of a hated viewpoint or belief—must compete for court time with more pressing issues. Judges may also set a high bar before treating the law as having been broken when it involves little more than expression of an offensive viewpoint.

Despite all the talk of "hate speech" on the left of politics in Western countries, the track record is typically that few such cases

---

17   'Reducing the backlog in the Crown Court', *National Audit Office*, 24 May 2024 (nao.org.uk/reports/reducing-the-backlog-in-the-crown-court).
18   B Chu and L Gilder, 'How many people are in prison and who is being released early from jail?', *BBC News*, 12 December 2024 (bbc.co.uk/news/articles/cd1jxmrk11yo).

are prosecuted—even where there would seem to be ample cause for concern that the speaker was inciting people to violence. The response in England to the riots in August 2024, where people were swiftly brought before the courts as a means of quelling the riots, are perhaps an exception. These exceptions aside, the failure to prosecute egregious cases of incitement to hatred under existing laws in some countries is arguably a greater problem than enforcement of laws directed towards suppression of speech that offends an interest group.

Regulatory authorities can also exercise judgements about which cases to pursue and how to do so. In a particular case, they might choose a punitive path with a church leader or a Christian organization in order to 'send a message'. However, taking a case to trial or arguing a matter on appeal can consume a lot of staff time and money. Agencies of this kind generally will not want to be seen pursuing political or 'culture war' agendas in deciding which cases to pursue at the expense of taking action over other serious matters.

Resource constraints and the independent decisions of prosecutors about which cases to pursue act as filters on which cases are likely to move forward from the very large number of offences that are reported to authorities. For the most part, the laws that are most likely to trouble law-abiding Christians rely on voluntary compliance. Christians can, responsibly, withhold voluntary compliance from laws that violate the human right to religious freedom in ways that cannot reasonably be justified. In so doing, we will often be holding governments to the values they profess. For at the present time, the governments and regulatory bodies that most loudly proclaim their commitment to human rights are often the most selective about the human rights they are prepared to uphold.

All this said, in deciding to breach the law, we risk detection (if the breach is covert) and punishment. That must be part of the decision-making equation, as it was for Daniel and his friends in Babylon so many centuries ago.

10

MOUNTING A LEGAL DEFENCE

When is a legal defence the right response?

There is very often a Christian case for settling disputes quickly (see chapter 8). There may also be a case for deliberate civil disobedience in which Christians risk being prosecuted. We should plead guilty when we do, because that is an aspect of our protest (see chapter 9). However, in other circumstances, there is a place for insisting on our legal rights. Paul's life illustrates this.

Paul's use of his Roman citizenship

Paul had the great benefit and blessing of being a Roman citizen. He was born a citizen (Acts 22:28), even though his origins were in the city of Tarsus rather than Rome (Acts 9:11). How he came to be born a Roman citizen is a mystery. He grew up as a devout Jew and was a member of a Jewish family. However, it was possible for citizens of Roman-controlled cities like Tarsus to acquire Roman citizenship as a reward for personal merit.[1] In some circumstances it could even be purchased, at huge cost (Acts 22:28). It may be that his father or another ancestor had been granted the privilege of citizenship.

Whatever the circumstances, Paul used his legal rights as a

---

1   TG Watkin, 'Paul of Tarsus: A citizen of no mean city', *The Journal of Legal History*, 1988, 9(2):119.

Roman citizen on various occasions. In Acts 16, it is recorded that Paul and Silas, both of whom were Roman citizens (v 37), were beaten and thrown in prison in Philippi. Paul didn't protest this at the time. God worked a mighty miracle that night: there was a violent earthquake, as a consequence of which the prison doors flew open and the prisoners' chains were loosened. Just as Paul might have avoided being flogged and imprisoned, so too he might have chosen that opportunity to escape (vv 22–34). Peter did so on another occasion, guided out of prison by an angel (Acts 12:1–11). Yet Paul and Silas stayed put.

We are not told why Paul and Silas made those choices. But we know that God "wants all people to be saved and to come to a knowledge of the truth" (1 Tim 2:4). The choices that Paul and Silas made led directly the conversion of the jailer and his household, as well as preventing the jailer from committing suicide after he thought his prisoners had escaped on his watch (Acts 16:27–34). In accepting suffering for the sake of bringing people to faith, Paul and Silas were following the example of their Lord.

However, after that time, when the magistrates ordered the release of the prisoners, Paul chose to rely upon his legal status as a citizen:

> Paul said to the officers: "They beat us publicly without a trial, even though we are Roman citizens, and threw us into prison. And now do they want to get rid of us quietly? No! Let them come themselves and escort us out." The officers reported this to the magistrates, and when they heard that Paul and Silas were Roman citizens, they were alarmed. They came to appease them and escorted them from the prison, requesting them to leave the city. (Acts 16:37–39)

By putting the magistrates on the defensive, Paul may have given them more reason than they would otherwise have had to protect Christian believers from the angry crowds.

Later, when in Jerusalem, Paul used his Roman citizenship to avoid being flogged. Having given his testimony of dramatic conversion on the road to Damascus, there were calls among the crowds for him to be killed. Paul was rescued from the mob by a Roman centurion commander, who ordered that he be flogged and interrogated in order to find out why he had enraged people. As the soldiers prepared to flog him, Paul asked the centurion: "Is it legal for you to flog a Roman citizen who hasn't even been found guilty?" (Acts 22:25). Paul knew the answer. So, in all probability, did the centurion. The interrogation and flogging were both abandoned (Acts 22:29).

Another time, in a hearing before the newly arrived Roman governor Festus, Paul used his legal right of appeal to the emperor to avoid being taken to Jerusalem to stand trial before the Jewish leaders there. It is questionable whether he would have made it alive to Jerusalem, given that the Jewish leaders had previously hatched a plan to ambush and kill Paul on the journey (Acts 25:1–12). Eventually, Paul would be put to death in Rome. However, this appeal to Caesar gave him some more years of writing and teaching ministry (Acts 28:16–31).

The New Testament record, then, shows Paul choosing when and how to rely upon his legal rights. He did not always do so. His account of the physical cost he sustained for preaching the gospel is evidence of how much he suffered for the faith, notwithstanding his Roman citizenship (2 Cor 11:23–27). However, he did not hesitate to invoke his citizenship at times.

We may find the need to insist upon our legal rights—both when the police come knocking, and if someone brings a lawsuit against us.

When the police come knocking

It may seem surprising that in a book written for Christians who ordinarily live law-abiding lives, there is a section on what to do when the police call. If what they are calling about is the alleged sexual abuse of a child, a domestic violence offence or something of that kind, there is no particular wisdom to impart. The law should take its course, and the accused, like any other member of the community, is entitled to offer whatever defence he or she can.

However, there is an increasing likelihood that Christians will find themselves having to respond to the police simply for expressing their views on contested social issues. There are now numerous laws in English-speaking countries that, in some way or another, criminalize giving offence to someone (see chapter 3). Typically, these laws are designed to protect people from offensive material that is based upon a protected characteristic such as their race or sexuality. Other laws make it a criminal offence to express viewpoints online that might incite 'hatred'. Governments may use such provisions to suppress discussion of difficult issues like levels of immigration.

Britain, for example, has laws that now make certain kinds of online speech a criminal offence, and police can use these laws in a very heavy-handed way to investigate and charge people for strongly worded expressions of opinion on certain 'hot button' issues.[2] Section 127 of the *Communications Act 2003* was discussed in chapter 1. Another broadly worded offence is section 1 of the *Malicious Communications Act 1988*. This provides that it is an offence for anyone to send another person a letter, electronic communication or article of an indecent or grossly offensive nature if his or her purpose is to cause distress or anxiety to the recipient or "to any other person to whom he intends that it or its contents or nature should be communicated".

To get a conviction under this section, the prosecution would need to show two elements. First, that the electronic communication could objectively be considered "grossly offensive". Second, that the purpose of posting it, or at least one of the purposes, was to cause distress or anxiety to someone to whom it was intended the post be communicated. It is not necessary to show that anyone was in fact distressed or made anxious.

Of course, this section applies to social-media posts, including reposting someone else's posts. The nature of X (formerly Twitter) and other such social-media services is that one cannot know who will see a public post. It may be amplified far beyond those who have

2   See, for example, E West, 'Britain isn't a free country', *The Spectator*, 23 January 2024 (spectator.co.uk/article/britain-isnt-a-free-country); A Creighton, 'UK crackdown on language turns free speech on its head', *The Australian*, 15 August 2024 (theaustralian.com.au/commentary/uk-crackdown-on-language-turns-free-speech-on-its-head/news-story/f321ea42eb68e8739773476480011b69).

chosen to follow the person originally posting. It follows that it may be difficult to show that the poster intended any particular person or group of people to see it. Prosecutions under this section require approval from a senior person in the Crown Prosecution Service.[3]

Notwithstanding the difficulties in achieving a conviction for social-media posts that may offend someone, there are stories from time to time of the police knocking on doors or inviting people for 'voluntary' interviews because they have posted a point of view online. Often, what triggers police action is when an individual is named or targeted, even if the post responds to something that the person has chosen to go public about.

Maya Forstater, a feminist who campaigns to protect women's single-sex spaces, posted on X about a GP who "enjoys intimately examining female patients without their consent". The GP is a man who identifies as a transgender woman. The context for the post was an article that Ms Forstater had written a few years earlier, responding to a news story about this doctor. In the article, she asked whether the doctor's patients were really empowered to say no to being intimately examined by a male, female-identifying doctor, if this view was seen as "prejudiced and ignorant". In so doing, she referred to various public statements that the doctor had made about intimate examinations of female patients. Ms Forstater did not tag the doctor in this post.

The police subsequently interviewed her for an alleged breach of the Malicious Communications Act.[4] She went public when, ten months later, she had still not been informed whether the police intended to lay charges, despite letters from her solicitor making representations about what the law said on this issue and pressing for a resolution.

The nature of most such cases involving social-media posts is that the police ought to know whether they are in a position to lay charges

---

3   'Communications offences', *Crown Prosecution Services* (cps.gov.uk/legal-guidance/communications-offences).

4   J Beal and J Ames, 'Police investigate activist who said trans GP enjoys examining women', *The Times*, 18 June 2024 (thetimes.com/uk/crime/article/police-investigate-activist-who-said-trans-gp-enjoys-examining-women-g8kvtm0vj).

after calling in the person for an interview, and perhaps talking with the person who is said to have been the intended recipient. There really isn't much further investigation they can do, even if they claim that a matter is still "under investigation".[5] Most likely such a long delay is because the file was sitting, neglected, in someone's in-tray awaiting a decision. Fifteen months later, and after advice from the Crown Prosecution Service, the police finally dropped the case.[6]

Cases of this kind illustrate how even posting on a matter of public concern—such as the right of women to know that a doctor listed as female is a biological male—can lead to police action being taken. Christians who engage in debate on such public issues can likewise be caught up in police inquiries, causing great stress, not because they are Christians, but because they choose to be involved on important social issues such as the rights of women and girls to single-sex spaces and bodily privacy.[7] Enough troubling cases seem to be reported out of the UK to suggest that the police, at least in some regions, need training on free-speech issues. They also need firm guidance on when a complaint indicates an issue that is serious enough to justify causing the anxiety and distress of a formal police investigation and an arrest.

However, if such an investigation is launched, the police inquiry might be sufficiently satisfied by a clear statement from the person accused that they had no intention to cause anxiety or distress of the kind that might justify a prosecution. In such cases, cooperation with the police may be the best option in difficult circumstances.

5   This was the claim of a Metropolitan Police spokesman, as reported by *The Times* (above).

6   F Attenborough, 'Police drop "terrifying" hate crime investigation into Maya Forstater', *Free Speech Union*, 16 November 2024 (freespeechunion.org/police-drop-terrifying-hate-crime-investigation-into-maya-forstater).

7   See, for example, the treatment of Caroline Farrow, director of Catholic campaigning website CitizenGo, who first experienced a police investigation after posting about the child of then Mermaids CEO Susie Green, an activist for the medical treatment of children who identify as transgender; A Lockhart et al., 'Moment police "with no search warrant" swooped on house of gender-critical Catholic mother and arrested her in front of her four children over "series of anonymous posts on internet chat board"', *Daily Mail*, 5 October 2022 (dailymail.co.uk/news/article-11282263/Moment-police-swoop-house-devout-catholic-mother-malicious-online-posts.html).

The right to remain silent

In other cases, a Christian may need to rely on his or her legal rights by remaining silent when interviewed by the police. That is a standard right in Western legal systems. When interviewing a suspect, police must tell him or her of this right and warn that anything the person says may be used in evidence against them. This is known as being interviewed under caution.

In December 2022, Isabel Vaughan-Spruce was arrested for praying outside an abortion clinic in Birmingham, England. This was allegedly in violation of a "Public Space Protection Order" made by the Birmingham City Council under section 67 of the *Anti-Social Behaviour, Crime and Policing Act 2014*. The Order prohibited certain conduct within the vicinity of an abortion clinic. The prohibited activity included "protesting, namely engaging in any act of approval or disapproval or attempted act of approval or disapproval, with respect to issues related to abortion services, by any means". This was said to include prayer.[8]

Ms Vaughan-Spruce was praying silently when three police officers approached her.[9] One of the police officers first cautioned her, and then asked her why she was standing there, given she did not live locally. She gave as a reason that this was the location of an abortion centre. Next, he asked her if standing there was part of a protest. She said 'no'. Evidently, she saw prayer as having a value other than as a form of protest. Next, he asked her "are you praying?". A truthful answer to that question might properly have been 'no', since at that moment she was talking to the police officer, not praying. However, she answered: "I might be praying in my head". He then asked her to accompany him to the police station voluntarily. She declined and was arrested. A judge later dismissed the case.

Ms Vaughan-Spruce was again arrested in March 2023, having acknowledged once more that she was engaging in silent prayer within the exclusion zone surrounding the clinic. The police officer

---

8   'Public Space Protection Order: Robert Clinic, Station Road B30', *Birmingham City Council* (birmingham.gov.uk/downloads/file/24121/robert_clinic_station_road_b30).

9   A video of the incident is on YouTube: 'Woman Arrested for Silently Praying' [video], *All Things ProLife*, YouTube, 23 December 2022 (youtube.com/watch?v=k6E105a58p8).

said this constituted the offence. Six months later, the police wrote to her saying she would not be charged and apologizing for the length of time it had taken to reach this decision.[10] Eventually, they had to pay her £13,000 in compensation.[11]

There was another option open to Ms Vaughan-Spruce in this situation: rely on her right to remain silent. She was entitled to give no answer as to whether she was praying. Nor, even if she did acknowledge this, was she under any obligation to tell police officers what she was praying about or whom she was praying for. That's none of their business. She was also entitled to offer no explanation as to why she was standing in that place. We can be polite and respectful to police officers without answering any of their questions. That is what the 'police caution' is all about. It actively invites suspects not to respond to police questioning.

Without answers, the officers would be left with evidence of a woman with known pro-life views standing near an abortion clinic, perhaps with her eyes shut, perhaps not. They would be unable to prove that she was praying rather than trying to remember the grocery list she had left at home. In such circumstances, prosecution would be foolish.

Under the current law in England, there are now 'safe-access zones' around all abortion clinics in the country.[12] To prove an offence, the prosecution would need to show that the person standing praying in a place within the safe-access zone was either intending to influence a person's decision to access or provide abortion services at the clinic, or to cause harassment, alarm or distress to them. The offence could also be proven if the person was "reckless" as to whether their conduct had this effect. In February 2025, it was reported that police had asked Ms Vaughan-Spruce to move on

10   S Caldwell, 'English police apologize to woman arrested for silently praying outside abortion facility', *Catholic Review*, 25 September 2023 (catholicreview.org/english-police-apologize-to-woman-arrested-for-silently-praying-outside-abortion-facility).
11   'Abortion clinic payout woman shocked at prayer arrest', *BBC*, 22 August 2024 (bbc.co.uk/news/articles/c4gze361j7xo).
12   Section 9 of the *Public Order Act 2023*.

from being in a safe-access zone, because, they said, her mere presence could cause "harassment, alarm, and distress". They argued that "people know who she is".[13]

In a situation where the prosecution's case is merely that the Christian intercessor was standing quietly within a safe-access zone, neither obstructing entrance nor communicating with people going in and out, the less additional assistance the accused person can give them the better. If the prosecution cannot even prove that she was praying, let alone that she intended to influence people going in and out of the clinic from accessing or providing abortion services, it would be very difficult to prove any element of this offence beyond reasonable doubt.

The right to remain silent, sometimes called the privilege against self-incrimination, extends to a criminal trial. The Fifth Amendment to the US Constitution makes this a constitutional right: "No person ... shall be compelled in any criminal case to be a witness against himself". There is no requirement for the accused person to give evidence by going into the witness box. Commonly, on legal advice, they do not do so because this will expose them to cross-examination by the prosecution lawyer. The prosecution must prove its case beyond reasonable doubt based upon the evidence it has gathered. The defence can seek to demonstrate a reasonable doubt in a variety of ways—by cross-examining the prosecution witnesses, by calling their own witnesses, or by positing to the judge or jury some other alternative explanation for the alleged crime. Such defences can be mounted without the accused giving evidence personally.

Shirts, coats and the case for vigorous defence of civil proceedings

We may also need to offer a vigorous defence when we are sued by someone using the civil law. As Christians, we are to be peacemakers —but we are not doormats. Jesus' advice in the Sermon on the

---

13 H Preston, 'Isabel Vaughan Spruce embroiled in another silent prayer controversy', *Premier Christian News*, 12 February 2025 (premierchristian.news/en/news/article/isabel-vaughan-spruce-embroiled-in-another-silent-prayer-controversy).

Mount was to settle disputes quickly and generously: "If anyone wants to sue you and take your shirt, hand over your coat as well" (Matt 5:40; see also v 25). It is usually in the best interests of anyone being sued to try to reach a settlement reasonably quickly before legal costs mount—at least when the compensation that might be agreed upon is modest compared to the legal costs of defending the dispute (see chapter 8). Businesses will often seek to settle disputes "on a commercial basis". That means they seek to reach the most prudent financial decision in the circumstances, whatever the merits of the case against them.

However, some claims brought against Christian organizations are vexatious or financially motivated. A case involving a Christian social-welfare organization in Australia provides an example. This organization only insists that staff be practising Christians at the senior executive level. Otherwise, it employs a great range of people without their faith being a criterion for appointment. A woman applied for an entry-level position and filed her anti-discrimination complaint before applications for the position had even closed. This made it obvious that the complaint was not made in good faith. Such claims need to be resisted.

For similar reasons, it may be necessary to resist, or at least question, some complaints of historic sexual abuse. Very often, the church or Christian organization will have good reason to accept the complaint as true. For example, the alleged offender may have been known to have abused other children; the complainant was at the school or a member of the church at the time; or a psychiatrist presents evidence of profound impact on the person's life, leading to adverse financial consequences. There will be other cases where it is legitimate to test the veracity of the claim, at least to the extent of reviewing a detailed account of the alleged offending behaviour in an affidavit and any corroborating evidence that might be available. Whenever opportunities present themselves in life to make a lot of money quickly, there will be those who are tempted to exploit that opportunity fraudulently.

Depending on the law in that jurisdiction, it may also be possible and appropriate to defend the case on the basis that the church organization itself was in no way negligent and had no reason to suspect that the offender was doing what is alleged. As Christians, we must find the balance between appropriate generosity to those who have been hurt and wariness about claims that, for whatever reason, are not legally sustainable.

Seeking to settle a claim may also not be the best option for Christians and Christian organizations when legal claims are being weaponized against them for ideological purposes. The problem is that almost invariably, such claims are brought not to satisfy a personal claim to have been harmed, but rather to change the organization's future practices. A Christian school, sued for alleged discrimination because of a student's gender identity, may be asked not only to apologize but to adopt new policies to the effect that any teenager's embrace of a new gender identity, however sudden or novel, should be affirmed. A school that accedes to such a demand gives away too much. It gives up the right to adopt a cautious pastoral approach informed by its beliefs about what is likely to be in the best interests of this child, and also to take into account the good of the student community as a whole. In other situations, litigation may be pursued as a means of persuading the organization to change their beliefs—or at least the public expression of them.

'Lawfare' is part of the activist playbook. It is unlikely that an organization that is authentically committed to Christian beliefs could find a basis for settlement with an organization that is fiercely wedded to incompatible beliefs. Of course, compromises might be found through good faith negotiations, and the opportunity for respectful compromises should always be explored.

While, for the reasons given, litigation, or defending litigation, is sometimes necessary, it is not a good means of trying to resolve disputes that are not legal in nature. Sometimes people go to courts seeking a ruling on issues that the court is simply not in a position to resolve. A judge cannot resolve theological disputes or arguments about science. He or she may have to consider such matters in seeking to resolve the case, but will typically try to find some narrow legal pathway through the dispute, avoiding pronunciations on matters on which the law itself has no view.

Challenging overreach

One role that litigation can play is to challenge the views of police or regulators who express an unduly broad opinion on what the law means. It is a common-law principle that Parliament is assumed not to be intending to diminish human rights unless there is clear language to the contrary. As the Chief Justice of the High Court of Australia explained it, statutes must be interpreted with the aid of "a presumption that Parliament does not intend to interfere with common law rights and freedoms except by clear and unequivocal language for which Parliament may be accountable to the electorate".[14]

Judges act as an important filter on the overreach of the police or government organizations. Many laws interfere with basic freedoms, such as freedom of speech and of assembly. Some of these laws, such as public order statutes in England, are broadly drafted. The police may, in good faith, seek to enforce such laws. But they may do so without being fully aware of the need to balance their commitment to enforcement against the importance of the rights that are thereby being infringed. Judges must balance these matters in their interpretation of what Parliament intended by the words used in the legislation.

One way for Christian organizations to approach the issue of legislation that could have a broad impact on religious freedom is to choose a realistic, but reasonably conservative, view of its scope. As we saw in chapter 7, often the reach of the law can be understood in terms of concentric circles. Based upon well-informed legal advice, the organization may conclude that some activities are clearly forbidden (the bullseye in terms of legislative purpose), some are probably forbidden, some may or may not be forbidden, and some are probably not forbidden. A Christian organization could take an entirely risk-averse approach by adopting the broadest possible view of the law's reach and cease any activity that might fall within that scope. A reasonably conservative approach would be to avoid activities that are clearly or probably forbidden (unless a conscious choice is made, for gospel reasons, to disobey), but if the demands of ministry justify it, to do things that may be forbidden.

14   French CJ in *Momcilovic v The Queen* [2011] HCA 34 at 43.

There is, of course, no need to announce all this to the world. It is usually best to fly under the radar wherever possible. But the organization must be prepared to defend the legality of its position in court if needed. It is then up to prosecutors or a regulatory authority, if they become aware of the activity, to take such action as they see fit. They might choose not to pick the fight, recognizing that their enforcement resources are better utilized to deal with clear breaches. If they decide to test the reach of the law in court, the worst-case scenario for the Christian organization is that the prosecutor wins the case. What may or may not have been forbidden previously is now in the 'clearly forbidden' category as a result of the court's ruling. But this worst-case scenario may not eventuate at all, or it may not eventuate for several years. If, instead, the Christian organization takes the most risk-averse approach, then it will obey the broad interpretation of the law from that moment on, stifling what may be appropriate and beneficial Christian ministry or legitimate free speech.

Of course, litigation for the purpose of clarifying the scope of the law involves risks. The result may be a very unfavourable interpretation that creates more difficulties than if the law had been left uninterpreted by a court. In litigation, as in other kinds of campaigning, it is important to pick our battles.

The importance of Christian legal defence organizations

The threat of civil litigation is intimidating for individuals and for local churches. It is often said that the process is the punishment. It costs the complainant nothing to lodge an anti-discrimination or 'hate speech' claim, and it is not uncommon for such complaints to be withdrawn at a later stage without resolution—and without cost to the complainant. In the meantime, the individual defendant or accused Christian organization has spent large amounts of time and money on legal fees, mounting a defence to the claim. The costs of so doing often far exceeds the level of compensation that would have been payable had the claim succeeded.

The threat of prosecution is also likely to be intimidating for most people. That is one reason why the law is effective in operating by persuasion rather than coercion. The legal costs of defending a prosecution that might result in a good-behaviour bond, or perhaps a fine, will sometimes be greatly in excess of the punishment itself.

What is clear, in a society where the law can be weaponized for ideological purposes, is that these problems will not go away. There is a need therefore to socialize the costs for churches and Christian organizations, just as insurance companies socialize the costs among a large number of insured. At an institutional level, that may indeed be done through insurance that provides comprehensive cover for potential liabilities to which the organization is exposed. For individuals, there is not the same possibility of socializing the risk of being a defendant in legal proceedings.

Christian organizations that specialize in legal defence and advocacy for Christians—such as the Alliance Defending Freedom in the USA (and its global arm, ADF International), Christian Concern in the UK, and the Human Rights Law Alliance in Australia—therefore play an important role in socializing the costs of fighting legal battles to protect religious freedom and freedom of conscience. They need financial support as well as the assistance of lawyers prepared to act *pro bono*.[15]

Such advocacy organizations often need to come to the aid of Christians who, people may consider, have acted unwisely or expressed their views without demonstrating grace. Defending them from criminal charges or in civil lawsuits does not need to involve support for all that they have said and done. Some sincere Christians choose the wrong hill to die on. They still need good Christian lawyers to defend them.

15   *Pro bono* means without charging fees.

11

RELIGIOUS FREEDOM IN A MULTICULTURAL SOCIETY

Can the liberal tradition of mutual tolerance survive?

The intrusion of the State into religious activities

If secularizing trends continue, there is some likelihood that Christians as individuals, and churches as organizations, will find increasing conflicts with the law's requirements. In a speech in May 2024, Anthony Fisher, Catholic Archbishop of Sydney, posited a scenario of what might happen:

> The year is 2035, hopefully my last as archbishop. I've just emailed my draft homily for Sunday to the Religious Safety Commissioner for her approval. She's the independent regulator charged with ensuring that faith groups spread no discriminatory and otherwise harmful messages. With the help of AI, she vets all planned sermons and spiritual talks to be given in Australia each week, catching any inappropriate words or themes before they are spoken.
>
> Our school system also meets each month with Departmental officials to monitor what's taught in our schools and ensure this accords with contemporary expectations. The Department itself now appoints Catholic school principals, SERECs (Secular Ethics and Religious Education Coordinators),

and other staff in accord with DEI policy and approves all curriculum.[1]

He went on to imagine other dystopian scenarios such as faith-based hospitals that are no longer able to operate because they will not perform abortions or support euthanasia. He envisaged that other faith-based community services could lose their charitable status.

Archbishop Fisher's scenario was, as he acknowledged, exaggerated for effect. However, the idea that the State might want to regulate what churches teach, and to whom, is not at all far-fetched. It arises from three trends.

The first trend is to believe that traditional moral teaching on sexual behaviour is antithetical to human flourishing. According to this view, no pleasurable sexual activity between adults should be frowned upon as long as it is consensual. That includes various forms of violent sexual practices as well as the production of pornography for adult use. Teachings that criticize lawful sexual conduct are offensive inasmuch as they challenge people's freely made choices about their bodies. They may even be 'discriminatory'.

A second trend is to take a very broad view of 'psychological harm', and to accept purely subjective claims of harm as a sufficient reason to shut down speech with which people disagree and that might be a source of such harm to them. This has been a reason given, for example, for trying to close down debate on issues concerning gender identity.[2] Any teaching that upsets people by expressing a negative view concerning certain kinds of sexual behaviour or relationship should, on this view, be outlawed as harmful. In particular, school students should be protected from harm. That is the kind of thinking that appears to have led to Bernard Randall (whose situation we discussed at length in chapter 3) being referred to the anti-terrorism police. His offence was to preach a mild chapel sermon to the effect that it is okay for students to

1   Fisher, 'Religious Freedom in a Secular World'.
2   H Siddique, 'Stonewall is at centre of a toxic debate on trans rights and gender identity', *The Guardian*, 5 June 2021 (theguardian.com/society/2021/jun/05/stonewall-trans-debate-toxic-gender-identity).

accept the Church of England's teaching on sexuality and gender issues.

A third trend is to accept no limits on the power of government to regulate religious organizations, including churches, synagogues and mosques. This marks an end to a recognition that there ought to be some kind of separation between Church and State, or, in Augustinian terms, that there are two cities—the city of God and the secular realm, each with their distinctive spheres of authority.

The traditional Christian understanding of the role of government is that it may regulate various aspects of the life of the church as a subset of the whole community for the common good. Child protection legislation is an example. However, it may not interfere in issues of doctrine, worship, discipline or church governance. The famous Westminster Confession, drawn up in London in 1646 as an expression of Reformed theology, has this to say on the relationship between the State and churches:

> Civil magistrates may not assume to themselves the administration of the Word and sacraments; or the power of the keys of the kingdom of heaven; or, in the least, interfere in matters of faith. Yet, as nursing fathers, it is the duty of civil magistrates to protect the church of our common Lord, without giving the preference to any denomination of Christians above the rest, in such a manner that all ecclesiastical persons whatever shall enjoy the full, free, and unquestioned liberty of discharging every part of their sacred functions, without violence or danger. And, as Jesus Christ hath appointed a regular government and discipline in his church, no law of any commonwealth should interfere with, let, or hinder, the due exercise thereof, among the voluntary members of any denomination of Christians, according to their own profession and belief.[3]

That separation between Church and State was also reflected in the American revolution. Thomas Jefferson, for example, wrote:

3   *Westminster Confession* 23.3.

Believing with you that religion is a matter which lies solely between man and his God, that he owes account to none other for his faith or his worship, that the legislative powers of government reach actions only, and not opinions, I contemplate with sovereign reverence that act of the whole American people which declared that their legislature should "make no law respecting an establishment of religion, or prohibiting the free exercise thereof", thus building a wall of separation between church and state.[4]

Such a division in roles is no longer fully accepted by some secular authorities. The encroachment on the autonomy of religious organizations has occurred largely by stealth. Originally, the argument was presented that organizations in receipt of government funds should be required to adhere to the government's non-discrimination policies, not only in terms of who the organization serves, but in how it is staffed.[5] Now, in some jurisdictions at least, broad-ranging anti-discrimination laws are applied to religious organizations with limited exemptions, irrespective of whether the organization receives public funds.

The undeclared war on religious teachings

Undoubtedly, much of the pressure on religious freedom has come from advocacy by groups seeking complete acceptance for homosexual relationships, including in faith communities, or recognition that those who identify as another gender are in fact the gender with which they identify. The law is increasingly invoked to try to drive

---

4   Letter to the Baptist Association of Danbury, Connecticut, on 1 January 1802.
5   See, for example, the submission of the Discrimination Law Experts Group on the *Exposure Draft of the Human Rights and Anti-Discrimination Bill 2012* (Cth). It argued: "As a matter of principle ... public funding should not be spent on any activities that are discriminatory". Submission no 207 to Senate Standing Committee on Legal and Constitutional Affairs, Parliament of Australia, Inquiry into the Exposure Draft of the Human Rights and Anti-Discrimination Bill 2012, December 2012, p 28 (aph.gov. au/Parliamentary_Business/Committees/Senate/Legal_and_Constitutional_ Affairs/Completed_inquiries/2010-13/antidiscrimination2012/submissions).

out or suppress dissent on such issues. This has placed some governments, or at least influential members of governments, in a state of undeclared war on traditional religious teachings. Christianity has been in the firing line because of its historic role in the formation of the Western tradition and because of its continuing, if declining, cultural influence. However, attacks on traditional Christian teachings equally affect the other Abrahamic faiths and the cultural values of many ethnic minority groups.

There may yet be some possibility of working out a peaceful accommodation on these issues. Whatever their views on the interpretation of New Testament references to homosexual conduct, churches have had to work through the pastoral issues involved when so many young people in particular now identify as same-sex attracted or 'gender diverse', or see themselves as 'allies' to those who are. Many same-sex couples in committed monogamous relationships express a genuine commitment to the Christian faith.

The weakening influence of the LGBTQ+ movement

At the same time, the LGBTQ+ movement is fracturing. Some lesbian and gay groups are distancing themselves from the transgender activist sectors of the movement.[6] The transgender movement is going backwards after astonishingly quick gains in changing law and policy around the Western world. The Executive Orders issued by President Trump in his second term, declaring that henceforth the United States will only recognize two sexes, and prohibiting the administration of puberty blockers or cross-sex hormones to those under 19 in federally funded facilities, have been a major blow to the transgender movement.

The prohibition of what is called 'gender-affirming care' for minors reflects a broader international trend. Some governments are now severely restricting the prescription of puberty blockers

---

6   See, for example, LGB Alliance (lgballiance.org.uk). See also C Moore, 'Why it's time for LGB to divorce T and Q', *New York Post*, 18 November 2023 (nypost.com/2023/11/18/opinion/why-its-time-for-lgb-to-divorce-tq).

and cross-sex hormones to minors.[7] More and more detransitioners are coming forward, deeply regretting their treatment and in some cases suing doctors and hospitals. Mostly, these are young women who had significant mental-health problems at the time of receiving cross-sex hormones or having a double mastectomy, and who were given treatment despite red flags concerning diagnosis and the capacity to give informed consent.[8]

The extent of the unfolding medical scandal could well do great damage to the credibility of LGBTQ+ advocacy organizations that have been promoting such sex trait modification treatments and arguing to make access to them easier. Much of the effort to pass 'conversion therapy' laws around the Western world seems to have come from a desire to portray gender identity as innate and unchangeable, and not a manifestation of psychological problems or neurodiversity. Arguably, these laws are directly responsible for many mental-health professionals now being unwilling to provide young people the support they need to explore their gender incongruence, open to the possibility that it may be a symptom of other unresolved issues in their lives. It follows from this that the LGBTQ+ advocacy organizations will be very directly implicated in the unfolding scandal.

The inclusion of males identifying as females in women's elite sports has also generated huge controversy, as a consequence of which some world sporting authorities have amended rules to ensure that no athlete who has gone through puberty as a male can compete in women's elite competitions. The Trump Administration has also addressed this issue with an Executive Order that will necessitate considerable changes in the practices of schools, colleges and sports bodies that have hitherto allowed trans-identified males to participate in female sports events and competitions.

It is likely also that LGBTQ+ identification will decline from current heights. Many who now identify as LGBTQ+ see themselves as

---

7   See, for example, the Cass Review in the UK (cass.independent-review.uk/home/ publications/final-report).

8   For a case against one of America's most prominent gender clinicians, see 'Children, Consent and Controversy: Clementine's Story', *The Center for American Liberty*, 12 December 2024 (libertycenter.org/cases/clementine).

'bisexual' or 'non-binary'. A study of the attitudes and experiences of adults in the USA over a period of more than 40 years found that while the number of American adults who had at least one same-sex partner since age 18 doubled between the early 1990s and early 2010s, almost all of that increase was in bisexual behaviour. There was little consistent change in those having sex exclusively with others of the same sex.[9] The US evidence is that bisexuality is quite common for young females, and many young women who report same-sex attraction go on to identify as only heterosexual a few years later,[10] entering into conventional heterosexual relationships.

Adolescents may now identify as 'non-binary', but that identification may prove transitory as people's normal sex drives and ticking biological clocks impact upon the way they understand themselves. In all probability, the current fashion for heterosexual young people to identify themselves as 'queer', based upon ever more finely grained distinctions concerning their sexual attractions or gender identity, will also pass.[11] Identifying with the large community of those who say they are LGBTQ+ gives alienated and socially isolated people a sense of meaning and belonging; but another generation of adolescents and young adults will find other ways to fulfil those needs. It is hard to think of any previous adolescent movement in which teenagers have adopted the same intellectual fashions or causes as their mothers.

LGBTQ+ advocacy groups have been at the forefront of campaigns for laws that remove religious exemptions or that can be weaponized against people of faith. However, for all these reasons, it is probable that their influence will diminish over time. The nature

9   J Twenge, R Sherman and B Wells, 'Changes in American adults' reported same-sex sexual experiences and attitudes, 1973–2014', *Archives of Sexual Behavior*, 2016, 45(7):1713–30 (doi.org/10.1007/s10508-016-0769-4).

10   M Ott et al., 'Stability and change in self-reported sexual orientation identity in young people: application of mobility metrics', *Archives of Sexual Behavior*, 2011, 40(3):519–32 (doi.org/10.1007/s10508-010-9691-3); N Dickson et al, 'Stability and change in same-sex attraction, experience, and identity by sex and age in a New Zealand birth cohort', *Archives of Sexual Behavior*, 2013, 42(5):753–63.

11   The website Healthline, for example, lists 68 different genders: '68 Terms that Describe Gender Identity and Expression', *Healthline* (healthline.com/health/different-genders).

of causes that identify themselves as 'progressive' or 'on the right side of history' is that they are constantly changing. This is not a new phenomenon. In Acts 17, Luke observed that Athenians and the foreigners who lived in Athens "spent their time doing nothing but talking about and listening to the latest ideas" (v 21). Paul urged the Ephesians to attain "the whole measure of the fullness of Christ" so that "we will no longer be infants, tossed back and forth by the waves, and blown here and there by every wind of teaching" (Eph 4:13–14). Those who are not firmly grounded in a faith or even a coherent philosophy of life are typically tossed around from one belief to another, sometimes struggling to keep up with the crowd.

Fertility, immigration and multiculturalism

Another trend that is likely to affect the direction of Western societies is the falling birth rate across the Western world (and indeed many countries in Asia, such as Japan and South Korea).[12] In most such countries, birth rates have fallen very far below population replacement rate.[13] Declining birth rates have a cascading effect. As fewer women have children, and as women who do have children have smaller families, there are simply fewer females around in the next generation to become mothers. So the cascading effect continues from one generation to the next.

However, the decline in fertility is not evenly distributed across populations in Western countries. A study of eight European countries found that practising Christians who regularly attend church services both intend to have, and succeed in having, more children than those who are not religious.[14] Similar trends are observable in

---

12 'What does the global decline of the fertility rate look like?', *World Economic Forum*, 17 June 2022 (weforum.org/agenda/2022/06/global-decline-of-fertility-rates-visualised).

13 On average, each woman needs to have 2.05 children during her fertile years in order for the population size to remain constant.

14 I Buber-Ennser and C Berghammer, 'Religiosity and the realisation of fertility intentions: A comparative study of eight European countries', *Population, Space and Place*, 2021, 27(6):e2433.

the United States.[15] The Muslim world has particularly high birth rates. Between 2010 and 2015, births to Muslim women made up an estimated 31 per cent of all babies born around the world. This far exceeded the Muslim share of the population in 2015, which was 24 per cent.[16]

With sharply declining fertility in western countries, the working-age population required to support increasingly ageing societies can only be maintained at current levels by quite large-scale immigration. This is not only to provide the workforce needed in areas such as health and aged-care services, but at a more general level to supply the tax base required to fund public services.

Apart from legal immigration to alleviate labour shortages, populations in Western countries are also growing as a result of significant population movement, with young men in particular crossing oceans and continents, fleeing dysfunctional countries and oppressive regimes or seeking better economic prospects.

While immigration patterns will vary from country to country, it is very likely that a substantial proportion of migrants will be devoutly religious. People in sub-Saharan Africa are the most likely to say that religion is very important in their lives. At least 90 per cent of adults say this in Senegal, Mali, Tanzania, Guinea-Bissau, Rwanda and Zambia.[17] Some 970,000 people migrated from sub-Saharan Africa to Europe as asylum seekers between 2010 and 2017.[18] Others will have come through normal migration channels, such as refugee resettlement and family reunification programs.[19]

15   L Stone, 'America's Growing Religious-Secular Fertility Divide', *Institute for Family Studies*, 8 August 2022 (ifstudies.org/blog/americas-growing-religious-secular-fertility-divide).

16   'The Changing Religious Landscape', *Pew Research Center*, 5 April 2017 (pewresearch.org/religion/2017/04/05/the-changing-global-religious-landscape).

17   J Evans, 'Where is the most religious place in the world?', *Pew Research Center*, 9 August 9 2024 (pewresearch.org/short-reads/2024/08/09/where-is-the-most-religious-place-in-the-world).

18   'At least a million Sub-Saharan Africans moved to Europe since 2010', *Pew Research Center*, 22 March 2018 (pewresearch.org/global-migration-and-demography/2018/03/22/at-least-a-million-sub-saharan-africans-moved-to-europe-since-2010).

19   Pew Research Center, 'At Least a Million Sub-Saharan Africans'.

Devoutly religious people are also likely to migrate to Europe or the United States from other parts of the world. Latin Americans are among the most likely in the world to say they pray daily.[20] In the Islamic countries of the Middle East and North Africa, from which so many migrants and refugees come, the proportion of the population that says religion is very important to them is also very high.

If these demographic patterns continue, with people of faith having much higher birth rates and migrating to Western countries in quite high numbers, then the religious will inherit the earth;[21] or at least, they will represent an ever-growing proportion of the population of countries that have most embraced secular belief systems.

This will put great pressure on today's anti-faith secularists. For as long as our societies have regular elections, governments will have to be responsive to the makeup of the population, and in particular the composition of marginal constituencies. If there are high concentrations of people of faith in enough marginal constituencies, it is likely this will affect how political parties view issues concerning religious freedom.

Loss of belief in the Western liberal tradition

The likely future for Western democracies over the long term, then, is that these societies will contain more people who are devoutly religious, relative to those who have no faith at all. This will be the case in those countries that are already highly multicultural and have long experienced high rates of immigration. Other countries without the tradition of absorbing migrants will struggle with plummeting birth rates and an ageing population, as Japan has experienced already.

However, having more devoutly religious people as a proportion of the community does not mean that belief in the Western liberal tradition will recover. This tradition, which has given us the freedoms

20   Evans, 'Where is the most religious place?'
21   E Kaufmann, *Shall the Religious Inherit the Earth?: Demography and Politics in the Twenty-First Century*, Profile Books, 2010.

that we have long enjoyed, is far from secure. It will be undermined by two factors. The first is a loss of belief among elites in the value of that tradition. The second is that new migrants will come mainly from countries that are not imbued with that tradition.

Nowhere is the loss of belief among elites more extensive than in the humanities faculties of America's top universities, where ideas such as critical race theory, queer theory and post-colonial theory are mainstream. These very different bodies of thought have one thing in common: hostility to the civilization which has been built up over centuries by people (mostly white, mostly male) imbued with values derived from Greek, Roman and Judeo-Christian thought (see chapter 5).

This new thinking is revolutionary inasmuch as the common thread is to criticize the liberal tradition as being inherently oppressive to various minorities. It is also said to be the cause of much harm to traditional societies through its export, as the European empires expanded their reach. The dominant theme of these intellectual movements is one of seeking to tear down and destroy the institutions that oppress, be that 'white supremacy' or 'cisheteropatriarchy'. Overall, these movements view the history of their countries as steeped in exploitation and oppression. Australian historian Geoffrey Blainey has called this the "black arm-band view of history".[22]

However, unlike other revolutions, this one has no discernible end goal, no vision for a better and different future or a better means of ordering society. There are those who call the ideas behind this movement the "successor ideology",[23] but it has no intellectual coherence or unifying idea beyond what it opposes. Nonetheless, a theme of the anti-liberal movement is a disdain for traditional freedoms such as freedom of speech and religion. Freedom is for those who think the right thoughts and say the right things. For others? Not so much.

There is a generational aspect to the loss of belief in Western

---

22   G Blainey, 'A Black Arm-Band for Australia's 20th Century?', *Upholding the Australian Constitution*, 2000, 12:110.

23   The term was invented by essayist Wesley Yang.

values. British think-tank UK Onward reported in 2019 that over a third of those under 35 supported the idea of having the army run the country. This was about three times the level recorded in a European Values Survey 20 years earlier. Conversely, only 76 per cent of this age group thought that a democratic system was a good way to run the country, while 64 per cent of under-35s supported having a strong leader who does not have to bother with Parliament.[24]

The loss of belief in Western values among those fortunate enough to have been born into these societies is compounded by the fact that few of the people who are likely to migrate to these societies will come from countries where Western values and democratic traditions are deeply embedded in the culture. They may be supportive of Western values such as the rule of law, but they will bring their own cultural values and ways of organizing community life that may be quite different from Western ways. Many will also have come from countries with authoritarian regimes.

In the long term, these demographic trends in Western societies may be significant, given the speed at which the composition of the population in some western democracies is changing. As of mid-2023, over 30 per cent of Australians were born overseas.[25] In New Zealand, the percentage is over 27 per cent,[26] and in the USA it is nearly 15 per cent.[27]

The combination of these factors means that over time, Western societies will have fewer and fewer people who have the same shared values and shared British or European cultural heritage. Of those who do, some will see those values and that cultural history largely in negative terms, as sources of oppression. That will make

24   W Tanner and J O'Shaughnessy, *The Politics of Belonging*, Onward, 2019.
25   'Australia's population by country of birth', *Australian Bureau of Statistics*, 24 April 2024 (abs.gov.au/statistics/people/population/australias-population-country-birth/latest-release).
26   Stats NZ, '2018 Census data allows users to dive deep into New Zealand's diversity', 21 April 2020 (stats.govt.nz/news/2018-census-data-allows-users-to-dive-deep-into-new-zealands-diversity).
27   SS Azari et al., 'The Foreign-Born Population in the United States: 2022', *United States Census Bureau*, April 2024 (www2.census.gov/library/publications/2024/demo/acsbr-019.pdf).

these societies particularly susceptible to shocks that could under-mine the very foundations of liberal democracies. That may in turn lead to authoritarian governments that have no time for ideas with deep roots in Christianity, such as the rule of law or human rights. If intercultural conflicts or anti-immigration protests become a reg-ular problem, religious faith may come to be seen in negative terms as a cause of community disharmony, justifying repression.

Shaping the future

The dystopian vision for the future just described is different from the one given by Archbishop Fisher, with which this chapter com-menced. Some version of both may come to pass. Nothing is inevitable.

As Christians now, we can help shape the future of the societies in which we live. Our societies may increasingly come to look and feel strange to us, much as the Jews must have felt when they were taken to Babylon. The Jewish exiles there were advised through the prophet Jeremiah:

> "Build houses and settle down; plant gardens and eat what they produce. Marry and have sons and daughters; find wives for your sons and give your daughters in marriage, so that they too may have sons and daughters. Increase in number there; do not decrease. Also, seek the peace and prosperity of the city to which I have carried you into exile. Pray to the LORD for it, because if it prospers, you too will prosper." (Jer 29:5–7)

False prophets had claimed that the exile would be over within two years and the king of Babylon defeated (Jer 28:2–4), but instead Jeremiah advised them that they would be there for 70 years.[28] In this context, Jeremiah said, the Jewish people needed to continue maintaining traditional family structures, raising children and grow-ing in number. They were also to seek the peace and prosperity of

---

28   P Colgan, 'Does Jeremiah 29 call us to seek the welfare of the city?', *GoThereFor.com*, 27 March 2017 (gotherefor.com/offer.php?intid=29593).

their society. There was, then, an internal and external dimension to living successfully in Babylon—an environment in which, as Daniel, Shadrach, Meshach and Abednego all found (Daniel 3, 6), there were life-threatening challenges to godly living. This is not to say that everything about our situation is identical to the Old Testament people of God in exile. But surely there are similarities. We are, after all, described as "God's elect", but also as "exiles" (1 Pet 1:1; 2:11).

The internal dimension is for the Christian church to be a model to the society around it in terms of family life and community well-being. For all the modern focus on new family forms, the reality is that heterosexual marriage and child-rearing in the context of heterosexual marriage play a central role in the preservation and long-term growth of the people of God.

For critics of the Judeo-Christian tradition, 'heteronormativity' needs to be smashed. That was the catchcry of the organization brought into Bernard Randall's Anglican school in Britain to train staff on issues concerning sexuality and gender identity (see chapter 3). But the truth is that heterosexuality is normal, and raising children within the context of a married heterosexual family unit is typically for the best. To thrive in our 'Babylon', we will need to hold fast, without embarrassment, to these fundamental Christian truths. We cannot be tossed to and fro by every wind of progressive doctrine (Eph 4:13–14).

Yet we live in societies where many people are struggling to find or maintain a lifelong heterosexual marriage. Many people who regularly attend Christian churches have experienced marriage breakdown or have been unsuccessful in finding a partner. Some have a settled same-sex orientation that prevents them from having an authentic intimate partnership with someone of the opposite sex. These are the pastoral realities of today's church life, in the context of a relationship drought in the wider society.[29]

The New Testament answer to this is to understand the church as the family of God, and for all faithful members of the church to

---

29   P Parkinson and M Jensen, 'The Relationship Drought: A discussion paper for church leaders', *Publica*, 14 July 2022 (publica.org.au/relationshipdrought).

see themselves as members of that greater family. As John wrote, to all who received Jesus, "he [Jesus] gave the right to become children of God" (John 1:12). Together, as God's children, we are brothers and sisters, members of the household of God (2 Cor 6:18; Gal 6:10; Eph 2:19). In Psalm 68, the psalmist describes God as a "Father to the fatherless, a defender of widows" who "sets the lonely in families" (vv 5–6). The church, at its best, can be a place of healing and redemption for all those who have experienced brokenness in our family life—and that is a great many of us.

The external dimension of living in 'Babylon' is to seek the peace and prosperity of the society. That won't be easy when Judeo-Christian civilization is experiencing a period of decline. But we can still contribute to that society in any number of ways through our work, and through what we do as neighbours and friends.

Some will be called to promote the peace and prosperity of the society in the public square. Lawyers and advocacy groups will need to play an important role in keeping the public square open to the gospel, and to maintain the capacity of Christians to engage in gospel-motivated contributions to community wellbeing through volunteering, adoption, fostering, and many other avenues.

In increasingly multicultural societies, it will be important for Christians to work together with people of other faiths to secure better protections for religious freedom and to seek to repeal or amend those laws that inhibit the free exercise of our faith.[30] This may mean playing a long game, because for now, the secularization trend in Western democracies seems entrenched. However, demography is destiny, as the great French philosopher Auguste Comte once said. On this basis, the outlook for anti-faith secular humanism is not promising.

Focusing on ultimate purpose

Seeking to preserve a tolerant society respectful of the right to freedom of religion, conscience, speech, assembly, and other such

---

30 Of course, there will be constraints upon the extent to which this kind of partnership is possible; but we may be able to find much common ground.

human rights is nonetheless not our ultimate purpose. These are means to an end. Paul wrote in his first letter to Timothy that we are to pray for "all those in authority, that we may live peaceful and quiet lives in all godliness and holiness"; this "pleases God our Saviour, who wants all people to be saved and to come to a knowledge of the truth" (1 Tim 2:2–4). The spread of the gospel is the end goal. Despite the difficulties arising from the increasing number of laws that restrict religious freedom or can be weaponized against people of faith, we need to keep our eyes fixed on Jesus (Heb 12:1–2), revering him as Lord (1 Pet 3:15), and resolving to "seek first his kingdom and righteousness" (Matt 6:33).

Laws that are (or might be) weaponized against people of faith may have some good purposes for the people of God. For example, laws that allow for complaints to police based upon what we say can at least act as a reminder that we should watch what we say— not to avoid legal trouble, but to avoid causing harm to our gospel witness. Yes, we must seek to defend truth in the public square, but that must be done with graciousness. Paul wrote to the Colossians: "Let your conversation be always full of grace, seasoned with salt" (Col 4:6). David prayed: "May these words of my mouth and this meditation of my heart be pleasing in your sight, LORD, my Rock and my Redeemer" (Ps 19:14).

Laws that prohibit discrimination can also remind us to follow Jesus' example in how we treat people. To those who would stone the woman caught in adultery, Jesus asked pointedly whether any of them were without sin. If so, they should cast the first stone— but no-one did (John 8:1–11). To the Samaritan woman he met at the well, he spoke gently and without condemnation, knowing that she had had five husbands, and that she was not married to her current partner (John 4:17–18). It seems she had not made a great success of the 'one man and one woman for life to the exclusion of all others' idea, although John tells us nothing more of her personal circumstances. Yet Jesus treated her with respect and dignity.

Laws that provide religious groups with charitable status remind us that religion is seen to be a public benefit, so long as the public are reached by our work (see chapter 2). That should encourage us to have an outward focus for our churches, and to find ways of bene-fiting the community beyond our doors.

Laws that provide other kinds of remedy for people who have grievances against us remind us to look beyond the problem to the person. The grievance itself may or may not be well-founded, but bringing that dispute out into the open, and having the opportunity to discuss it through mediation, provides a means by which we can reach out in love to that other person, sympathetic to their personal needs and emotional struggles.

This is not to say that seeking to live and to respond to conflict in a Christlike way will prevent us from having legal problems. It was not so for Jesus himself, and he warned his disciples that they might find themselves in similar circumstances:

> "Be on your guard; you will be handed over to the local coun-cils and be flogged in the synagogues. On my account you will be brought before governors and kings as witnesses to them and to the Gentiles. But when they arrest you, do not worry about what to say or how to say it." (Matt 10:17–19)

Just prior to this, he had advised the disciples to be "wise as serpents and innocent as doves" (Matt 10:16, ESV). Innocence is good. We also need wisdom.

Feedback on this resource

We really appreciate getting feedback about our resources—not just suggestions for how to improve them, but also positive feedback and ways they can be used. We especially love to hear that the resources may have helped someone in their Christian growth.

You can send feedback to us via the 'Feedback' menu in our online store, or write to us at info@matthiasmedia.com.au.